"An important book for those who seek true happiness, and doesn't everybody?"

—**John Bradshaw,** personal growth expert; author,
Healing the Shame That Binds You

"An inspirational guide that everyone can use. Profoundly wise, combines practical steps to take and uplifting stories. A must read."

—**Dr. Barbara Becker Holstein,** happiness coach; author,
The Enchanted Self: A Positive Therapy and *Recipes for Enchantment, the Secret Ingredient Is You!*

"Provides us with an understanding of our spiritual side…. It's like a conversation with a warm and trusted friend."

—**Betty Ford,** former first lady; founder,
Betty Ford Treatment Center

"This thought-provoking book brings together insights from Torah and psychotherapy to challenge us to reflect on how to live a meaningful life. Through reflection on important questions like 'What is it that God wants of me?' it does indeed present a formula for proper living."

—**Rabbi Laura Geller,** senior rabbi,
Temple Emanuel, Beverly Hills

"Much more than studying genetic factors, set points, or diet prescriptions, Dr. Twerski's simple examples and entertaining explanations make reading this book a happy and life changing event."

—**Judi Hollis, PhD,** author, *Hot & Heavy: Finding Your Soul through Food and Sex* and *From Bagels to Buddha*

"I defy anyone to read this book and not become kinder, more spiritual and insightful. For people of all faiths, and of none, by one of the great Jewish teachers of our age. If you want to be a blessing in the lives of those around you, and in your own life, read this book."

—**Rabbi Joseph Telushkin,** author,
A Code of Jewish Ethics and *Jewish Literacy*

"A detailed presentation of the aspects of the unique human spirit will smooth the path for undertaking ten steps to happiness. Gentle humor and subtle stories will weave their way into your life. This appreciation of spirituality will make anyone want to pursue that goal ... and learn how better to do so."
—**Ernest Kurtz, PhD,** coauthor, *The Spirituality of Imperfection: Storytelling and the Search for Meaning*

"Exceptionally well-written, thought-provoking ... discusses the need in all of us to lead meaningful lives."
—**Robert J. Ackerman, PhD,** author, *A Husband's Little Black Book: Commonsense, Wit and Wisdom for a Better Marriage;* and *A Wife's Little Red Book: Commonsense, Wit and Wisdom for a Better Marriage*

"Wonderful ... explains what we are missing and how to achieve it. Filled with stories and written in a direct, personal way ... could well help people to find nothing short of meaning and happiness."
—**Elliot N. Dorff, PhD,** author, *The Way Into* Tikkun Olam *(Repairing the World)*

"Brilliant.... Shows how happiness and spirituality are intertwined and achievable. Simply reading this joyful writing will put you on the road to happiness."
—**Rabbi Berel Wein,** founder and director of The Destiny Foundation; author, *Triumph of Survival*

"Written with clarity, compassion, comics and practical wisdom ... harvests a lifetime of spiritual study, psychological counseling and life experience guiding us to be our best and our happiest."
—**Rabbi Elie Kaplan Spitz,** author, *Healing from Despair: Choosing Wholeness in a Broken World*

"Puts into words the yearning we all feel to live fully with joy and happiness. Helps us on our journey by gently teaching the heart and guiding the mind as we journey toward a life of greater contentment."
—**Karyn D. Kedar,** author, *The Bridge to Forgiveness: Stories and Prayers for Finding God and Restoring Wholeness*

A Formula for Proper Living

ALSO BY DR. ABRAHAM J. TWERSKI
FROM JEWISH LIGHTS

Happiness and the Human Spirit:
The Spirituality of Becoming the Best You Can Be

A FORMULA for PROPER LIVING

Practical Lessons from Life and Torah

Abraham J. Twerski, MD

For People of All Faiths, All Backgrounds

JEWISH LIGHTS Publishing

Nashville, Tennessee

A Formula for Proper Living:
Practical Lessons from Life and Torah

2009 Hardcover Edition
© 2009 by Abraham J. Twerski

Library of Congress Cataloging-in-Publication Data

Twerski, Abraham J.
  A formula for proper living : practical lessons from life and Torah / Abraham J. Twerski.
      p. cm.
  Includes bibliographical references.
  ISBN-13: 978-1-58023-402-3 (hc)
  ISBN-10: 1-58023-402-X (hc)
  ISBN-13: 978-1-68336-543-3 (pbk)
  1. Jewish way of life. 2. Spiritual life—Judaism. 3. Self esteem—Religious aspects—Judaism. 4. Self-perception—Religious aspects—Judaism. 5. Self-realization—Religious aspects—Judaism. I. Title.
  BM723.T7845 2009
  296.7—dc22

                                                                                    2009032213

10   9   8   7   6   5   4   3   2
Manufactured in the United States of America
Cover design: Melanie Robinson
Cover art: © Dmitri MIkitenko—Fotolia.com

Published by Jewish Lights Publishing
A Division of Longhill Partners, Inc.
An Imprint of Turner Publishing Company
4507 Charlotte Avenue, Suite 100
Nashville, TN 37209
Tel: (615) 255-2665
www.jewishlights.com

CONTENTS

ACKNOWLEDGMENTS

I am deeply grateful to Emily Wichland, vice president of Editorial and Production at Jewish Lights Publishing, for her superb editing and organizing of this book, adding to it substantively as well as formally.

Many thanks, too, to Stuart M. Matlins, founder and publisher of Jewish Lights; Michaela Powell, project editor; and all of the staff at Jewish Lights for making this book possible.

INTRODUCTION

There is an ancient story that a desert king, who had heard of the greatness of Moses, sent his artists to the Israelite encampment to make a portrait of him. When they returned, the king submitted the portrait to his physiognomists, who were able to deduce a person's character from his facial features. The physiognomists reported that the portrait was of a selfish, narcissistic, ego-driven, jealous, and lustful person. Inasmuch as this was the polar opposite of what he had heard about Moses, the king went to see for himself.

Upon meeting Moses, the king saw that the portrait had been accurate to a fault. When he told Moses of the physiognomist's interpretation, Moses explained that physiognomists can determine only the traits with which a person was born. "They were correct," Moses said, "because I was indeed born with all those negative traits. However, I transformed them into positive traits, directed toward a spiritual goal."[1]

---

1. Cited by *Tiferet Yisrael,* end of *Kiddushin*.

Moses's process of transformation is what Talmudist Rabbi Elijah ben Shlomo Zalman, known as the Vilna Gaon, called "breaking one's traits." A human being comes into the world as a biological creature, with all the traits that are inherent in other living things. It is the obligation of the human being to transform these traits so that they lead to the goal of a close relationship with God.

In modern times, we may call this transformational process a formula for proper living, an understanding of the human body, mind, and spirit that can guide us to achieving a sense of balance and spiritual well-being. For some, this formula may seem elusive. We rush out to meet the flood of new self-help material and gurus that is developed each year based on their promise of health, wealth, and happiness. With each new crop of theories and approaches, our hope is renewed that we will find the fix we need to finally achieve healthy relationships and lasting spiritual well-being. Yet each program seems to fall flat after the media buzz subsides and the trend is declared dead.

But if we look closely at Torah—the Hebrew Bible and supporting Jewish wisdom literature—we will find all the material we need to live righteously—and humanly—in relationship with God. Within the pages of this book, I will show that when taken together, the Torah supplies a complete formula for proper living that accounts for your human ability to choose as well as the inner workings of the human mind that can affect how you make your choices. I will also show you that the effectiveness and timelessness of the Torah's formula for proper living are proven to us again and again, as modern psychiatry and medicine present theories as "new" only to find their roots based in Torah.

Wisdom from Torah Can Equal Personal Growth

To begin, in chapter 1 I will explore what drives us as human beings and Torah's insights on these formidable forces. A human being is a composite creature, composed of a body, which is essentially an animal body, and a number of traits that animals lack, which, taken together, compose the human *spirit*. Unlike animals that are dominated only by biological drives, we can use our intellect to determine how we wish to live. In effect, we have the ability to choose. However, our choices are influenced by inherent instincts for both good and evil—the *yetzer tov* and the *yetzer ra*—as well as conscious and unconscious motivations. These can obscure the way for choosing the right path.

The choices we make are significantly affected by how we view ourselves—our identity—and how we feel about what we see—our self-esteem. In fact, identity and self-esteem form the core of humanness. In chapter 2, I will examine the importance of establishing an accurate self-awareness—complete with strengths, weaknesses, and potential to improve—and the stealthy ways that self-destructive feelings and actions can undermine our ability to make healthy choices and sabotage our spiritual well-being.

Our identity and self-esteem also play key roles in our relationships with others. As critical as it is to proper living to generate self-love and respect, it is equally important to love and respect those with whom you interact. In chapter 3, I will look at what it means to be made in the likeness of God (*Pirkei Avot* [Ethics of Our Fathers] 3:18) and how the simple—and sometimes not-so-simple—acts of giving and receiving can help us form lasting bonds and fulfill the sacred mandate to love others as ourselves.

Even our best intentions for living righteously and respect-fully can get derailed, and most frequently the derailments are caused by the work of our own minds! In chapter 4, I will expose some of the most common unconscious defense mecha-nisms that can be counterproductive to our pursuit of proper living. Rationalization, projection, denial, narcissism, anger—these are vehicles for our persistent evil instinct to throw us into self-destructive patterns. As you will see, in most cases the only effective course of action is to be aware and alert to such defense mechanisms and address them as soon as they appear.

Adversity is another force that tends to push us off track. Illness, socioeconomic meltdown, emotional upheaval, mourn-ing—no one escapes these challenges completely. Such events can grossly distort our thinking and cause us to act out of char-acter. In chapter 5, I will discuss the various ways that Torah guides us in controlling how we react to adversity through pur-pose, community, hope, and perseverance.

Improving our character traits helps us fulfill the divine mandate to repair the world. We cannot expect to fulfill the purpose of creation—to manifest God's presence in the world—by defying the morality and ethics endowed to us in the divine spirit. In chapter 6, I will examine the responsibility we have as human beings, our God-given abilities to master our inclinations, and the steps we can take to right wrong actions. By keeping our purpose first and foremost in our minds, we can generate rich and happy memories that will sustain us our entire lives.

What's Guiding Us?

Throughout this book, I primarily draw from the wisdom and teachings of the Torah, the Talmud, the writings of the

Jewish ethical movement known as *mussar*, and Chassidic writings.

"Tanakh" refers to the Five Books of Moses—Genesis, Exodus, Leviticus, Numbers, and Deuteronomy—as well as the biblical books known as Prophets and Writings. The Talmud, literally "the learning," is the great Jewish compendium of law, wisdom, folklore, and everyday life compiled by Sages in Babylonia and in Israel from the fourth century BCE to the fifth century CE. Accessories to the Talmud are the many commentaries from the latter date up to the present.

The Jewish ethical writings are teachings that combine religious philosophy, psychology of religion, devotional preaching, and ethics to address self-discipline. In the mid-nineteenth century, Rabbi Yisrael of Salant launched the *mussar* (ethics) movement in Lithuania. Rabbi Yisrael felt that although the Talmud was rich in ethical teachings, it was necessary to formalize courses in ethics, emphasizing refinement of character traits. The concept of *mussar* was ancient, promulgated by the great works of ethics such as *The Gates of Repentance* (*Shaarei Teshuvah*) of Rabeinu Yonah ben Abraham Gerondi, the *Kuzari,* written by Yehudah HaLevi, *The Duties of Heart* (*Chovat Halevavot*) by Rabeinu Bachya ben Joseph ibn Pakuda, and *The Ways of the Righteous* (*Orchot Tzaddikim*) (author unknown). Although these works were always studied by Torah scholars, Rabbi Yisrael felt that the time required formal courses of ethics in the seminaries. In their writings and lectures, Rabbi Yisrael and his disciples formulated and popularized the study of ethics, with the goal that a person should be in control over his or her thoughts and feelings rather than be controlled by them. *Mussar* necessitated a thorough understanding of the human intellect and affects. Just as secular psychology seeks to maximize a person's happiness and functioning, *mussar* sought to maximize a person's *spiritual* happiness and functioning.

The Chassidic writings stem from the mid-eighteenth-century revival movement in Eastern Europe called Chassidism, founded by Rabbi Yisrael ben Eliezer Baal Shem Tov. (My father is a ninth-generation descendant of the Baal Shem Tov.) At that time, Jews in Russia and Poland were oppressed by anti-Semitic regimes. They were disenfranchised, restricted from living in large cities and from entering the professions. Most Jews lived in smaller towns and villages, eking out a meager livelihood, and were subject to pogroms. Several decades earlier they had been disillusioned by Sabbatai Zvi (1626–76), who claimed to be the Messiah and attracted a huge following of those hopeful of redemption from misery. These circumstances resulted in a generalized despair among Jews. Because of their oppressed conditions, many Jews did not have adequate access to Torah education. The scholars formed an elite group, and the simple folk, sincere and devout in their observance of Judaism, felt further discriminated among their own. The Baal Shem Tov preached a message of hope and joy. Every Jew was dear to God, being required only to serve God according to the best of their ability. Hence the unlearned person, sincere and dedicated in worship of God, was no less important than the most learned scholar. Being a dear child of God was adequate reason for a person to rejoice, even if material circumstances were poor. This uplifting message struck a welcome chord, and the Chassidic movement proliferated.

As mentioned earlier, I also draw from the work of modern psychiatry, psychology, and medicine to show that new discoveries in behavioral science are not necessarily new. Sigmund Freud, the father of psychoanalysis, was trumped in his theory of unconscious motivation by Torah's instructions for observing Shabbat. Carl Jung, also a significant force in the development of psychoanalysis, was bested by Rabbi Shneur Zalman of Liadi, the author of the foundational Chassidic text the *Tanya*, on his theory of the collective unconscious. Even the Twelve Steps of Alcoholics Anonymous, the powerful and empowering recovery approach of Alcoholics Anonymous, founded by Bill Wilson and "Dr. Bob" in 1938, were preceded by principles introduced two thousand years earlier in the Talmud.

My Beginnings with Torah's Formula

As mentioned earlier, I am the son of a Chassidic rabbi. My father had a huge following in Milwaukee and was an intuitive counselor par excellence. His study was constantly buzzing with people who sought his guidance. He had a way of working with adverse litigants, bringing resolution to some very thorny cases, which led to his receiving a citation from the judiciary. Judges were known to say, "Take this case to Twerski."

From childhood on, my aspirations were to emulate my father. I received the traditional seminary education in preparation for the rabbinate and was ordained in 1951, to serve as assistant to my father in his congregation.

Following World War II, psychiatry and psychology had a meteoric rise, and it soon became clear to me that I would not be able to function like my father. The cloak of counseling had been lifted from the shoulders of the clergy and placed on the shoulders of the mental health specialist. Pastoral counseling had not yet come into its own. I saw that my function as a rabbi would essentially be to conduct services and perform religious rituals, such as weddings, funerals, and bar mitzvahs.

This was not to what I had aspired. Conducting ceremonies seemed so superficial and was not fulfilling for me. I felt that in order for me to function as my father did, I would have to don the cloak of a mental health professional. With my father's blessing, I entered Marquette University Medical School and received my MD degree. After a year of internship in general medicine, I received psychiatric training at the University of Pittsburgh Western Psychiatric Institute.

Much later, I realized that my father's keen counseling abilities were not simply due to his intuitive mind. Rather, his intuitive mind made use of the rich Torah education and heritage that he possessed, fashioning Torah knowledge into a formula for proper living. Early in my career, when I was asked whether I was applying any of my rabbinical training in psychiatry, I naively said, "No." Eventually, I came to realize that the Torah teaching I had received had a profound impact on how I related to clients and their problems.

Here is an example of applying Torah wisdom to psychiatric practice. I learned much about Sigmund Freud's theory of dreams and how to use dream interpretation in therapy. The Torah relates the dream of Pharaoh of Egypt, who dreamt of seven fat cows being devoured by seven thin cows (Genesis 41). Pharaoh's soothsayers interpreted the dream as meaning that he would bear seven children and that seven children would die, or that he would conquer seven countries and lose seven countries, but Pharaoh rejected these interpretations. Joseph then interpreted the dream to mean that there would be seven years of plenty followed by seven years of famine, and he advised Pharaoh to store the produce of the seven years of plenty to be available during the years of famine. Pharaoh not only accepted Joseph's interpretation, but also appointed him viceroy of Egypt to implement his plan.

Why was Joseph's interpretation more acceptable to Pharaoh? Because whereas the soothsayers predicted what would happen, they did not suggest any solution to what they predicted. Joseph included a solution to the problem posed in the dream. That taught me that in order to get a client to accept my interpretation of his or her problem, I must provide the client with a solution.

There was much that I learned from anecdotes that my father related. For example, he told of our great-uncle, the Chassidic rabbi of Talna, who was receiving his supplicants who sought his counsel and guidance for their problems. After several hours of responding to their petitions, the rabbi's aide noted that his clothes were saturated with perspiration. Since the room was not particularly warm, he said to the rabbi, "Why were you sweating so profusely? You were not exerting yourself physically."

"I was not exerting myself?" the rabbi responded. "You must understand that when someone presents a problem to me, I cannot advise him unless I thoroughly understand the problem and how it is affecting him. In order to do this, I must identify with him. I must take off my clothes, as it were, and put on his clothes. However, once I have identified with him, I can no longer evaluate the problem objectively, because I am influenced by all the feelings that influence him. To regain my objectivity, I must take off his clothes and put on my clothes. For the past several hours, I have been repeatedly taking off my clothes, putting on others' clothes, taking their clothes off and putting on my clothes, and you say that I have not been exerting myself?"

In all my psychiatric education, I never came across a better model of an effective therapeutic relationship. If the therapist does not identify with the client, the therapist's help is limited. If the therapist does identify with the client but fails to regain objectivity, the therapist cannot be of much help. The therapist must, therefore, master the technique of identifying and detaching, not a small feat.

I was taught that I would often not know the solution to a client's problems and that very often the client had the solution but was unaware that he or she had it. If I would listen attentively, it is likely that in relating the problem, the client would discover the solution. The trick, however, is to listen attentively. As Moses said, "Any matter that is too difficult for you, you shall bring to me and I shall hear it" (Deuteronomy 1:17). Moses never promised that he would solve their difficulties, but that he would listen.

In Pursuit of the Perfect Spirit—Wisdom for People of All Faiths, All Backgrounds

While my background and the sources used in this book are primarily drawn from Judaism, the insights on character development that you'll encounter throughout are accessible to people of all faith traditions. As you will find in the pages ahead, Torah is filled with the very practical knowledge we all are seeking in order to live properly and spiritually. It is a joy to be able to share it with you. As your entryway, I wish to lead you with a prayer attributed to Maimonides, the great twelfth-century codifier of Torah law and famous physician of antiquity, which spoke to me:

> *Before I begin the Holy Work of Healing the creation of Your hands, I place my eternity before the throne of Your glory, that You grant me strength of spirit and fortitude to faithfully execute my work.*

Let not desire for wealth or benefit blind me from see-ing truth. Deem me worthy of seeing in the sufferer who seeks my advice a person—neither rich nor poor, friend or foe, good man or bad; show me only the person.

If doctors wiser than I seek to help me understand, grant me the desire to learn from them, for the knowledge of healing is boundless. But when fools deride me, give me fortitude. Let my love for my profession strengthen my resolve to withstand the derision even of people of high station.

Illuminate the way for me, for any lapse in my knowl-edge can bring illness and death upon Your creations. I beseech You, merciful and gracious God, strengthen me in body and soul, and instill within me a perfect spirit.

1

WHAT DRIVES US?

The Talmud relates that when Moses ascended to heaven to receive the Torah, the angels protested to God, "Do not give the Torah to mortals. They are incapable of observing it. Leave the Torah here with us."

"Can you rebut their argument?" God asked Moses.

As his response, Moses asked the angels, "The Torah says, 'You shall not covet your neighbor's wife.' Does that apply to you?"

"No," the angels replied.

Moses continued, "The Torah says, 'You shall not steal.' Does that apply to you?"

"No," the angels replied.

By showing the angels that the laws of the Torah cannot apply to them, Moses succeeded in bringing the Torah down to earth.

The message in this Talmudic tale is that we were given the laws of the Torah precisely because we have the impulses and urges that the Torah seeks to manage. In short, we were given the Torah because we are not angels.

Instincts for Good and Evil

> And God caused to sprout from the ground every tree that was pleasing to the sight and good for food ... and the Tree of Knowledge of Good and Bad.
>
> GENESIS 2:9

Even the most virtuous people are confronted with desires for good and evil on a daily basis. Twelfth-century Jewish philosopher Nachmanides gave us insight into this by explaining that just as animals each have their natural instincts, humans were created with an instinctive nature, with only a very weak potential to deviate from our natural instinct. Had we retained our original nature, all human behavior would have been good, and we would not have had to use reasoning to distinguish good from evil. It was eating from the forbidden fruit that extenuated our natural instinct for doing good. Thus, according to Nachmanides, we are by nature good, but we have the potential to do evil. With dedication to being what we were intended to be, our good deeds could far exceed our bad deeds.

Modern psychiatry delves deeper into Nachmanides' theory. Sigmund Freud, founder of the psychoanalytic school of psychology, conceptualized the human mind as being comprised of the *id*, *ego*, and *superego*. The *id* refers to all instinctual drives. A newborn infant, self-centered and demanding immediate satisfaction, is pure *id*. But as the child matures and is subjected to parental discipline and social norms, she develops an *ego* that recognizes the constraints of reality and restrains the *id*. Then as the child internalizes parental and social morals and ethics, she develops a *superego*, which is essentially what we refer to as conscience.

The *ego* functions according to the reality principle, whereas the *id* functions according to the pleasure principle. For example, a man has a strong desire for an item in a store but either does not have the money or refuses to spend the money to buy it. Following the pleasure principle, he has the urge to take it (*id*). However, there are surveillance cameras and prominent signs that shoplifting will be punished to the full extent of the law. The *ego*, operating according to the reality principle, says, "If you give in to the *id* you may end up in jail." The man doesn't take the item. The restraint of the *id* is an *ego* function.

If, however, that same man finds a wallet with money, and no one saw him pick it up, the *ego*, operating within the reality principle, cannot restrain the *id* because there will be no consequences to him keeping the money. However, the *superego*—his conscience—steps in and says, "If you behave dishonestly, I will torment you." To avoid the anguish of the *superego*, the man looks at the identification card and returns the wallet to its owner.

The Talmud and later ethical works describe this inner struggle as a dyad: the *yetzer tov*, the instinct to do good, and the *yetzer ra*, the instinct to do evil. For all intents and purposes, the *yetzer ra* is Freud's *id*. The term "*yetzer ra*" should be understood not as being inherently evil, but rather as the source from which evil actions may emerge if the drives of the *yetzer ra* are not properly channeled. Maimonides, one of the most influential figures in medieval Jewish philosophy, said that without the *yetzer ra*—the source for hunger, acquisitiveness, and sexual drive—people would not marry, have children, or build homes. Unfortunately, we allowed the *yetzer ra* impulses to become dominant, as the Torah says, "The product of the thoughts of his heart was but evil always" (Genesis 6:5).

The Talmud recognizes that the *yetzer ra*—the *id*—is essential for life. In a picturesque passage, the Talmud relates that the Sages "trapped and imprisoned" the *yetzer ra* but had to release it because "one could not even find a fresh egg in the marketplace" (*Yoma* 69b). Rashi, in his authoritative commentary, explains that all physiology is dependent on the *yetzer ra*, and without it, life would be impossible.

Inasmuch as the essential life-drives originate in the *yetzer ra*, it is the function of the *yetzer tov*, our inclination to do good, to harness the energies of the *yetzer ra* and direct them toward positive goals. Interestingly, it is this yoke on our inclination to do evil that delivers us the freedom of happiness.

In Search of Freedom

> Proclaim liberty throughout the land.
>
> LEVITICUS 25:10

"Give me liberty or give me death." These are the immortal words of Patrick Henry that we learn in elementary school. Our national symbol is the Liberty Bell. Liberty is clearly a valued condition in our lives. It is important to also bear in mind, however, the words of the Pledge of Allegiance: "with liberty and justice for all." Liberty must be accompanied by justice. Liberty requires a sense of responsibility. Reckless abandonment, throwing off all restraints, is not liberty.

The Talmud presents an interesting debate between Rabbi Yehudah HaNasi, compiler of the Mishnah, and the Roman satrap Antonine about when the *yetzer ra* (evil inclination) enters a human being. Rabbi Yehudah said that it enters right at the moment of conception. But Antonine rebutted, "That cannot be. If the fetus had a *yetzer ra*, it would kick its way out of the mother's womb. Therefore, it must be that the *yetzer ra* enters at the moment of birth." The Talmud states that Rabbi Yehudah conceded to Antonine (*Sanhedrin* 91b).

Why would the *yetzer ra* cause the fetus to kick its way out of the womb? The womb provides it with an idyllic existence. All its needs are met. The fetus has no idea that there are pleasures in the world that might entice him. Furthermore, leaving the womb prematurely would mean certain death. Why would the *yetzer ra* prefer that?

The nineteenth-century Jewish ethicists of the *mussar* movement answer that the primary motivation of the *yetzer ra* is not, as is generally assumed, the pursuit of pleasure. What the *yetzer ra* wants is to be free of all restraint. Although intrauterine existence is idyllic, the womb is confining, and the *yetzer ra* prefers death to being confined and restricted in any way. Yes, if the fetus had a *yetzer ra*, it would kick its way out of the womb, even to certain death, rather than have an idyllic existence but be confined. Inasmuch as we all have a *yetzer ra*, it is important that we understand what its drive is. It wishes us to reject all authority and not tolerate any restrictions on our behavior, even when they are to our own benefit. The *yetzer ra* will push us to self-destruction just to be free of all restraint.

The *yetzer ra* is to us what alcohol is to the alcoholic. Those who understand the nature of alcoholism refer to alcohol as being a cunning, baffling, and powerful enemy. Just as this enemy uses all its powers to drive a person to absolute self-destruction, so does the *yetzer ra* use every trick to get its way. For example, when a child is told not to do something, that is precisely what the child may do, because the innate tendency is to defy control.

Rabbi Chaim Shmuelevitz (1902–79), dean of students of Mirer Yeshiva, Poland and Jerusalem, cites a biblical source for this. King David's son Absalom led a rebellion against his father, and David had to flee from Jerusalem. As he fled, a man named Shimi hurled vile curses against David. When the rebellion was quelled, David returned to Jerusalem, and Shimi pleaded to David to spare his life, extracting a promise from David that he would not kill him. Before David died, he told his son Solomon that despite the promise, Shimi deserved to be killed for cursing the king. David said, "*Use your wisdom* to see that Shimi does not die a natural death" (1 Kings 2:9; italics mine). When Solomon ascended to the throne, he ordered Shimi not to set foot outside of Jerusalem, and that if he did so, he would be killed. When two of Shimi's slaves fled, Shimi left Jerusalem to retrieve them, and Solomon had him killed (1 Kings 2:36–46).

Rabbi Shmuelevitz said that Solomon indeed used his wisdom because he knew that by forbidding Shimi to leave Jerusalem, that is precisely what he would do. Hundreds of people never left Jerusalem, but Solomon knew that human nature would make Shimi disobey his order.

The liberty that Patrick Henry sought and that we revere is not the freedom sought by the *yetzer ra*, but rather freedom with responsibility. We champion "liberty and justice for all," and "for all" includes both ourselves and others.

Unconscious Motivation

> If the intention is not pure, the deed is not acceptable.
>
> BACHYA IBN PAKUDA, *DUTIES OF THE HEART*

To fully appreciate the formidable force that is our *yetzer ra*, we have to understand the workings of our unconscious, that is, what is beyond our conscious awareness. Even though we are not consciously aware of the content of our unconscious, it can have significant influence over our actions.

One morning at services, I learned that a friend of mine had lost his mother and was observing the week of mourning (*shivah*) at his home. This was the last day of the *shivah* and my last opportunity to make a condolence visit. However, I had a patient scheduled shortly, and I knew that she was already en route to the office.

Not showing up for the appointment was unconscionable. I could explain things to my friend, but this bothered me as I drove to the office.

As I mulled over my options, I suddenly discovered that I was near my friend's house. I could have sworn that I was driving to my office, because that was what I wanted to do. But obviously a part of me wanted to visit my friend, and that part of me won out.

(As it turned out, just as I was to enter my friend's house, my cell phone rang. It was my patient reporting that traffic was at a standstill and that she could not make the appointment. I guess God sided with my unconscious.)

What seemed like unintentionally ending up at my friend's house is an example of what Sigmund Freud called unconscious motivation. When this concept was first introduced in the nineteenth century, psychology underwent a radical change. Freud proposed that we may do things without knowing why we are doing them, and even if we are not aware of the reason for our behavior, there is a reason that is beyond our awareness, that is, in the unconscious.

It is interesting to know how Freud came by this idea. Freud was attending a demonstration of hypnosis by world-famous hypnotist Ambroise Liebeault in Nancy, France. Liebeault hypnotized a subject from the audience and gave him the suggestion that after he would awaken and return to his seat, at a given signal, he would stand up and open his umbrella. However, he would have no memory that this suggestion had been given to him while under hypnosis. This is a classic posthypnotic suggestion.

After emerging from the hypnotic trance, the man returned to his seat, and Liebeault continued with his lecture. A few moments later, he made the gesture that was to serve as the signal. The man promptly stood up and opened his umbrella. Liebeault asked him why he had done something so absurd as to open his umbrella indoors, and the man said that he could not explain his action. He just had an urge to do it, even though it made no sense to him.

"Did anyone instruct you to do it?" Liebeault asked.

"No," the man answered.

The audience was probably amused by this demonstration, but Freud was much more than amused. He realized that there *was* in fact a reason why the man opened his umbrella indoors. He had been instructed to do so. But if he could not remember the instruction, how could it motivate his action? It must be that ideas of which a person is totally unaware, or that are in the part of the mind that is *unconscious*, can affect a person's behavior. From there on, it was only a matter of elaborating this concept.

Freud was a scientific thinker. He could not accept that anything happens without a cause. Inasmuch as he did not believe in God, he could not accept that anything was caused by God. However, he would have agreed in principle that a person who believes in God may ascribe causation to God. What Freud could not accept was that there were "accidental" happenings that occurred *without any cause*.

This led to his famous *Psychopathology of Everyday Life*, from which we derive the term "Freudian slip." Freud argued that if a person tried to unlock his office door and found that he had "accidentally" used the key to his house, that this mistake had meaning. That is, although *consciously* he wanted to enter his office, in his *unconscious* he wanted to be home. It was this unconscious ideation that caused him to use the wrong key. Freud claimed that every "mistake" has some meaning.

This was indeed a novel concept. The psychology profession at the time generally assumed that we do things because we have a reason for doing them and that we know what the reason is. The idea of unconscious motivation broke new ground and was not widely accepted.

But was this really new ground? Some three thousand years earlier, the Torah stated that if a person committed a sin unintentionally, he had to bring a sin offering to gain forgiveness (Leviticus 5:17). To help clarify this instruction, suppose a person has been traveling, lodging in a different motel every night. Friday night, back at home, he awakens in the middle of the night, has no idea that it is Shabbat, and puts on the light. He has committed a sin of violating Shabbat. Why is he held responsible for his act if he was not aware that it was Shabbat? Because the Torah holds a person responsible for actions of which he or she is not conscious—in other words, for behavior that was motivated unconsciously!

The Challenge of Being Human

One is not poor unless they lack knowledge.

BABYLONIAN TALMUD, *NEDARIM* 41

My knowledge of the unconscious that I acquired through Torah study preceded my psychiatric training and came in handy in avoiding unnecessary course work that would have been costly in time and money. As budding psychiatrists, my classmates and I were expected to undergo psychoanalysis to address unconscious ideation, meaning ideas and feelings that reside beyond our conscious awareness. By becoming aware of these unconscious ideas, we could avoid any distorting influences they may have on our actions and perceptions. Undergoing psychoanalysis would enable us to become aware of our unconscious feelings, many of which exist—or are repressed—in the unconscious because they make us uncomfortable and we want to disown them.

The mandatory psychoanalysis involved five sessions a week for several years and was costly even at the reduced rates given to psychiatric residents. I told my mentor that I did not need to undergo psychoanalysis because I was aware of the feelings that I had in my preconscious mind—that is, what I am not aware of at this moment but can become aware of if I wish to—and that they had not been relegated to the unconscious. My mentor said that this could not be so, that we all have ideas and feelings we cannot accept as belonging to us.

"There are 365 prohibitions in the Torah," I explained to my mentor. "We Jews believe that at Sinai, when God said, 'I am the Lord, your God,' God was speaking to each individual, including those not yet born. Thus, I personally was enjoined to observe all 365 prohibitions. If any of them were impossible for me, then in that respect, I would be like the angels, for whom the Torah is irrelevant.

"The Torah forbids murder, incest, and many other abominable acts that are abhorrent to me and that I don't think I am capable of doing or even remotely desiring. But if they are not within the realm of possibility for me, why would the Torah have forbidden them? I can only conclude that even though these acts are anathema to me, the desire to do them must exist somewhere within me, which is in my unconscious mind. So, you see, I don't need psychoanalysis to reveal to me the ideas that exist in my unconscious. It is my challenge as a human being not to act on them, but I do not need to disown them."

My mentor, perhaps reluctantly, agreed with me. Then he said, smilingly, "Perhaps it is better that you do not undergo psychoanalysis. You see, in psychoanalysis, someone must undergo change. In your case, the change might occur in the psychoanalyst instead of in you."

Subverting Our Evil Inclinations

> For I love him [Abraham], because he instructs his children and his household after him that they keep the way of God.
>
> GENESIS 18:19

If negative forces exist in our unconscious, is it possible that there are positive forces as well? Rabbi Shneur Zalman of Liadi, author of the basic Chassidic text the *Tanya*, says yes. He states that in every Jew there is a nucleus of love for God that was bequeathed by the patriarchs. He cites the phenomenon that during the Spanish Inquisition, Jews who were not committed to Judaism chose martyrdom rather than renounce their faith. Inasmuch as they did not practice Judaism, why did they choose death rather than reject a faith that apparently was not a serious consideration for them? Rabbi Shneur Zalman concludes that the inherited nucleus of love for God, although deeply buried and thickly concealed, nevertheless expressed itself when they were asked to renounce God.

The concept that ideas can be transmitted by heredity was one of the points of contention between Sigmund Freud and Carl Jung. Freud believed that all repressed material consisted of ideas and feelings that occurred as a result of events experienced by the person, but because they were unacceptable, these ideas and feelings were repressed and relegated to the unconscious mind. Jung argued that there are strong similarities among the content of the unconscious of different people, and that some repressed material is universal. It is highly unlikely, Jung said, that the same kind of unacceptable ideas and feelings occur to everyone; people don't have the same experience base. Therefore, Jung concluded, there are ideas and feelings that do not arise from experience, but are rather *inherited.* Inasmuch as such ideation is ubiquitous, Jung referred to it as the "collective unconscious," a term that was poorly understood when first introduced. In contrast to the individual unconscious, which consists of ideas and feelings that the person repressed, the ideation in the collective unconscious was not initially repressed by the person. Rather, it is ideation that exists in the mind because it was transmitted by heredity. In other words, repression did not *put* the ideation into the unconscious. Rather, repression *keeps* the hereditarily transmitted ideation from coming to conscious awareness.

The logic in favor of Jung's concept that there is hereditarily transmitted ideation is convincing. According to
Freud, a newborn infant does not have an unconscious. This
develops only as a result of experience. Inasmuch as it is the
superego that prevents access of certain ideation to the conscious mind, repression should not occur until the *superego* is
well developed. Yet, there is reason to believe that infants do
have an unconscious mind and that there is unconscious
ideation that exists before the *superego* has had a chance to
develop.

Preceding Jung by more than a century, Rabbi Shneur
Zalman posited that there is unconscious ideation that he
called *ahavah mesuteret,* or the concealed love for God that
every Jew has inherited from the patriarchs. This is a function of the Jewish *neshamah* (soul); hence a person who con-
verts to Judaism and acquires a Jewish *neshamah* has a
concealed love for God. The reason a person is unaware of its
presence, as noted above, is that such awareness would obli-
gate the person to a particular lifestyle and cause him or her
to feel guilty if its principles were transgressed. Under certain circumstances, such as when a person is coerced to
renounce God, the *ahavah mesuteret* emerges from the
unconscious, and the individual may consciously choose
martyrdom. This may also be a reason for the recent *baal-
teshuvah* phenomenon, with scores of people who were not
observant of Torah and some who had embraced Eastern
religions becoming interested in traditional Judaism and
attending yeshivot and seminaries.

Jung did not disagree with Freud that repressed material
can influence a person's behavior. This is true of the *ahavah
mesuteret.* People may act in a way that brings them closer to
God, even though they may not have an inkling why they are

acting this way. This is the effect of the *ahavah mesuteret* exerting its influence from its presence in the unconscious mind.

So while the hungers of the *yetzer ra* that exist in our unconscious can affect our actions negatively, the concealed love of God that also exists in our unconscious can affect our choices and actions positively. Knowing we have this concealed love for God within us should stimulate us to ask, "What is it that God wants of me?" This can be our guide to proper living.

2

IDENTITY AND SELF-ESTEEM

Your identity is determined by the set of characteristics by which you are known. These include your physical characteristics—male, female, tall, short, athlete, musician, scholar—as well as your spiritual characteristics—your capacity to give to others, your capacity for compassion, your commitment to justice. Your knowledge of these characteristics is what is known as your self-awareness. How you feel about these characteristics—personal respect for your goodness and talents—is your self-esteem.

When any of these factors regarding your identity are compromised, so too is your ability to live properly. It stands to reason, you can hardly make healthy adjustments to reality if your perception of reality is distorted.

Cartoonist Charles Schulz illustrated the effects of faulty perception masterfully in a cartoon that shows a little girl standing at the window, looking out at a bright, sunny day. Next to her is a little boy who is standing in front of the blackboard, saying, "Wow! Is it ever dark today." If that boy misperceives and thinks the blackboard is a window, he will indeed see the world as being dismally dark. Trying to convince him by logical argument that the world is bright and sunny is futile; his sense experience cannot be overridden by logic. To correct the misperception, we must take him to a window and point out to him that he had been looking at a blackboard. Only when he perceives reality correctly will he be able to adjust to it properly.

People can have similar experiences about their own identities. There are people who are attractive, bright, personable, and talented, yet for some reason, often unknown, they see themselves as unattractive, dull, unlikable, and inadequate. They are looking at the blackboard; to them, this view of themselves is reality. They are certain that anyone who looks at them will see them as unlikable, as they themselves do. Why would anyone looking at a heap of trash see a beautiful rosebush?

In the biblical account of the spies sent by Moses to scout Canaan, the Torah states that they returned with a foreboding account of its inhabitants. "And there we saw a race of giants. We felt like grasshoppers, and that is how we appeared to them" (Numbers 13:33). Rabbi Yitzchak Meir of Gur (1799–1866), founder of the Gur Chassidic dynasty, cited this verse and commented, "The Torah is telling you that the way you feel about yourself is the way you feel others perceive you" (*Otzar Chaim*, Numbers, p. 72).

Seeing the Complete Picture

> Someone who does not know his own worth—
> how can he estimate that of another?
>
> JAAKOB JOSEF FROM POLONIA

Developing an authentic identity is contingent on an accurate self-awareness. It is crucial that you are aware of your character strengths, as well as your weaknesses, in order to get a complete picture. The ethicist Rabbi Yeruchem Levovitz said, "Woe unto him who is not aware of his character defects, because he does not know what he must correct. But much worse is one who is unaware of one's character strengths, because he does not know that he has the ability to improve himself" (*Marbitze Torah*, 13). Without the complete picture, you are left with a faulty sense of who you are—you're looking at the blackboard—or no identity at all. Both conditions are fraught with problems.

If you lack an identity of your own, you may allow yourself to be identified by other people; that is, you may try to be whatever you feel others want you to be. You are then at the mercy of others, having no will and goals of your own. Evelyn was a bright young woman who didn't view herself as a competent person other than being a caretaker for her family, a role her mother assigned to her. She never invested any time in herself—she did not further her education or develop hobbies and interests of her own—because she didn't think she was worth it. She focused entirely on meeting the needs of others and fulfilling what they expected of her—first caring for her siblings, then for her own children. When her husband developed heart disease, she devoted herself to his care. When he died, Evelyn had no one to care for. Because she had not recognized her own potential, she had never developed it. With the loss of her identity as a caretaker, which was all she had, she went into a severe depression.

The importance of developing your own identity is best expressed by the Chassidic master Rabbi Menachem Mendel of Kotzk, who said, "If I am I because I am I, and you are you because you are you, then I exist and you exist. But if I am I *because* you are you, and you are you *because* I am I, then I do not exist and you do not exist" (*Truth Emits from Kotzk*, 566). In other words, if you are dependent on others to define you, you indeed exist as a physical entity, but you cannot be said to exist as a person.

A person lacking an identity may also seize upon external features for an identity, and this is equally problematic. One man's identity may be the Jaguar in his driveway; a woman's identity, the "MD" after her name. They define themselves by their wealth and status. The fragility of an external identity is well illustrated by a story of the wise men of Chelm, whose unique folly sometimes demonstrates significant psychological concepts.

A Chelmite was in the public bathhouse, and it occurred to him that without clothes, many people are indistinguishable. "When it comes time to go home," this Chelmite thought, "how will I know which one is me?"

He then had a bright idea. He found a piece of red string and tied it around his toe. Now he was distinct and had an identity.

In the process of bathing, the string fell off his toe, and when another bather stepped on it, it clung to his toe. When it was time to go home, he looked at his toe but saw nothing. Then he noticed the other man with the red string on his toe. He went over to this man and said, "Pardon me. I know who you are, but can you tell me who I am?"

If my identity is the Jaguar in the driveway, does the next owner of this Jaguar become me? If my only identity is the "MD" after my name, then it is the red string, and I am essentially indistinguishable from thousands of other physicians.

The Future Factor

> Who does not increase, decreases.
> PIRKEI AVOT (ETHICS OF OUR FATHERS) 1:13

An accurate identity is more than who you are at this very moment. Self-awareness also encompasses your potential—who you can be. Upon awakening, Jews pray, "God, the soul that You have put within me is pure." In the description of the creation of man, the Torah says that "God blew a breath of life into his nostrils" (Genesis 2:7). The *Zohar*, the foundational text of Kabbalah, the Jewish mystical tradition, points out that when a person exhales, he breathes out from within himself. Thus when God "blew" a breath of life into man, something of God entered man, and that is the human soul, which is godly (*Tanya*, chapter 2). Indeed, the psalmist says, "You made man just slightly less than angels" (Psalm 8:6).

Unlike God, who is omnipotent and infinite, you have a finite physical body that houses your soul and restricts and limits its powers. Despite these constraints, you have strengths and abilities far greater than you believe. Indeed, psychoneurologists say that we use just a fraction of our brains. But with this potential comes the responsibility to fulfill it. Ignoring your capabilities—that is, choosing to be unaware of your potential—may be an attempt to absolve yourself from that responsibility.

A twenty-four-year-old woman was admitted for treatment of alcoholism. She asked whether it would be possible for her to undergo psychological testing because she was concerned that she might have sustained brain damage due to her drinking. I assured her that she had not suffered any brain damage.

During her hospitalization, she persisted in asking for an electroencephalogram (brain wave study), CAT scan of the brain, and any other test for brain damage. I was puzzled why she could not accept my assurance, but it eventually became evident that she wanted to have a diagnosis of brain damage! Why? Because this would relieve her of all responsibilities. She could then say, "Don't expect me to stay sober, to hold a job, or to go to college. I don't have the ability to do so. I'm brain damaged."

Awareness of your abilities and strengths should not be mistaken for vanity and should not make you feel superior to others. Your personality assets are divine gifts. Indeed, awareness of your abilities should result in humility. Rabbi Yisrael of Salant said, "I know that my mind is equivalent to a thousand others, therefore my responsibilities are a thousand times as great."

Identity encompasses our abilities and strengths now and in the future. A healthy self-awareness places responsibility on us to live up to that potential. Failure to acknowledge our true selves and exercise our potential may be comfortable in one way, but it is a form of denying ourselves of who we are and may result in chronic unhappiness. Actualizing our potential, however—embracing our identity now and who we can become—can be most conducive to our happiness and spiritual well-being.

The Self-Defeating Cycle

> See, I have placed before you today life and
> prosperity, death and adversity.... I have placed
> life and death before you, blessing and curse.
>
> DEUTERONOMY 30:15, 30:19

Self-esteem goes hand-in-hand with an accurate identity when it comes to spiritual well-being. This is true, in part, because a negative or faulty self-awareness may lead you to actions that are not true to who you truly are—or can be. When you have an erroneous, negative self-concept, you can get stuck in a cycle of destructive, self-defeating behaviors that consistently derail your self-respect and that preclude you from developing your potential and becoming all that you can be. The result is low self-esteem. To stay in this cycle means spiritual well-being and self-fulfillment are unattainable.

What drives this destructive behavior, and why is it so common?

Sigmund Freud postulated that in every person there are two opposing instincts: *eros*, the survival instinct, which is a positive instinct that yearns for love, unity, and companionship; and *thanatos*, a negative death instinct, which leads to various destructive behaviors.[2]

Some two thousand years before Freud, the Talmud made a similar, remarkable conclusion: "A person's *yetzer*

---

2. Some of Freud's disciples rejected the *thanatos* theory, saying that when Freud postulated this theory, he was old and had undergone several operations for cancer of the palate. They felt that Freud was depressed and that the idea that every person has a death instinct was a result of his depression.

[evil inclination] grows in strength every day and seeks to destroy him" (*Kiddushin* 30a). As we learned in the previous chapter, the *yetzer* is an instinct or a drive, an integral part of every human being. Thus, every person has an instinct that seeks to destroy him or her, and this instinct—Freud's *thanatos* and the Talmud's evil inclination—is responsible for a variety of destructive behaviors. The awareness of this instinct is important in understanding human behavior and in countering low self-esteem.

Instincts are extremely powerful and can overwhelm logical thought. The saying "Love is blind" holds true because of the powerful force of *eros*, the survival instinct, which will push aside anything that stands in the way of pursuing its goal. It can cause a person to rationalize and to justify any behavior that will satisfy a given yearning.

The distorting capability of an instinct is true of *thanatos*, the death instinct, as well. Many self-destructive behaviors— including addictions to alcohol, drugs, nicotine, food, gambling, and sex—are due to this instinct. These are behaviors that people understand as self-defeating and may even want to stop, yet they are driven to continually do them. Other self-destructive behaviors are seen in people who act in ways that precipitate their being rejected or that regularly sabotage any project they undertake. Some people repeatedly enter into self-defeating relationships, especially marriage, where they seem to have a predilection for choosing abusive partners.

A board-certified pediatrician was admitted for treatment of alcoholism. I was amazed that this excellent person's self-esteem was below zero. When I asked her to tell me some of her positive features, she could not think of anything to say. Her record showed that she had graduated *summa cum laude* and had been elected to the Phi Beta Kappa honor society.

"You cannot deny that you're bright. They do not give Phi Beta Kappa honors to dummies," I said.

She sighed and said, "When they told me I'd been elected to the Phi Beta Kappa Society, I knew they'd made a mistake!"

She had married a ne'er-do-well who did nothing but lie on the couch and watch television, while she supported the family in addition to caring for their three children. He would berate her and criticize everything she did, and she believed it. That is how destructive low self-esteem can be!

The Powerful Effects of Inferiority

> Who is a powerful person? One who subdues one's personal inclinations, as it is said, "He who is slow to anger is better than a strong person, and a master of one's passions is better than the conqueror of a city" (Proverbs 16:32).
>
> PIRKEI AVOT (ETHICS OF OUR FATHERS) 4:1

Another manifestation of the death instinct is the lust for power, which has probably brought more destruction to the world than all the epidemics combined. People who suffer from low self-esteem may find relief in wielding power over others. They often overcompensate for feelings of inadequacy and inferiority with petulance, arrogance, and an unrelenting compulsion to fulfill their idea of success. This is as true of a school bully as of a dictator. The feeling of power may also give a person an illusion that he or she is beyond restraint, hence he or she can do anything he or she wants to.

The craving for power is particularly toxic in family relationships. Husbands and wives who try to exert power over each other or over their children undermine a wholesome family ambience. Power is incompatible with love; it breeds resentment rather than love. Although power-hungry persons certainly want to be loved, they are incapable of thinking of others—essential in all healthy relationships—because the desire for power overwhelms them.

Alvin was the managing partner of a large law firm, which he ran with an iron fist. Nothing was more important to him than his own ego, and in order to feed it, he sought ultimate control of everything within his power. If meetings were not held according to his plans, he would erupt in rage. If a colleague presented an idea that differed from his own, he would overrule it before his colleague could finish explaining. He exerted the same kind of authority at home as well. He had a devoted wife and two children who stood in awe of him, but they distanced themselves from him to avoid his angry outbursts. He belittled any work his wife pursued, no matter how charitable, and stifled his children's creativity by demanding that he always knew best. Although he craved love, he essentially sacrificed any chance of receiving it in his pursuit to sate his unquenchable thirst for power.

While the pursuit of power may convince a person they are beyond restraint, the Torah defines "powerful" quite differently. Moses referred to God as all-powerful. When the prophet Jeremiah witnessed the destruction of Jerusalem by the Babylonians, he no longer referred to God as all-powerful. Where is God's power if enemies can destroy God's Temple and exile God's people? The Sages of the Great Assembly answered, "That is the greatest manifestation of God's power, to see God's Temple destroyed and God's children exiled, and to restrain from acting" (Babylonian Talmud, *Yoma* 69b).

It is much easier to subdue others than to subdue our own drives, and it is much easier to be master over others than over ourselves. The message of the Talmud is that when you are master over your passions, you do not have to dominate others. The truly powerful people are those who, like God, can subdue their inclinations.

I have firsthand experience of the effects of feelings of inferiority and low self-esteem. As a fledgling rabbi, I was a member of a panel comprised of senior rabbis in the community. Because I felt inferior to them, I proceeded to upstage them. I doubt that this went over well with the audience, and I am certain I did not earn the affection of the older rabbis.

The reality was that although I was bright and talented, and in due time my skills would be appreciated, my feelings of inferiority, which were a distortion of my own reality, caused me to be impetuous and arrogant. I was not behaving in concert with my true identity.

Because of low self-esteem's delusional nature, it is difficult to convince a person that his or her negative self-concept is erroneous, thus ensuring the repetition of self-defeating behavior and sealing low self-esteem's cyclical trap. Just as a paranoid will refute every argument against his delusion, so may a person with low self-esteem be unable to accept many of his positive traits and may be unable to see that his negative self-perception is illusory.

Defeating the Death Instinct

Let not the mighty person boast of his might.... One may only boast of coming to know Me, and to emulate Me as loving-kindness, justice, and righteousness.

JEREMIAH 9:22–23

Though we all possess the death instinct, we need not fall prey to it. The Talmud was well aware of the intransigence of the *yetzer ra*, and says that it can be overcome only by divine help. But in order to secure that divine help, we must do our share. The Torah empowers us, saying that "God will bless you in all your handiwork that you may undertake" (Deuteronomy 14:29). Having struggled with low self-esteem myself, I developed a ten-step series of statements that, when reflected upon, can help counter the death instinct's assault on self-esteem. First published and elaborated on in my book *Ten Steps to Being Your Best: A Practical Handbook to Enhance Your Life in Every Way* (Shaar Press, 2004), the ten statements are as follows:

Step 1: I admit that I have a low regard for myself, that I do not value myself adequately and that I do not think I have much to offer others.

Step 2: I am entitled to regard myself as having value and worth because I was created by God and endowed with a godly soul. Therefore, I have unconditional value and intrinsic worth just by "being," independent of doing and accomplishing.

Step 3: My desire and need for approval from other people creates within me an unhealthy dependency.

Step 4: My adoption of a low self-esteem outlook on life has direct negative impact on my forming positive, wholesome bonds of intimacy with those in my inner circle. My adoption of a negative and pessimistic script with which to view my life blocks my achievement of happiness.

Step 5: I gain personal benefit and a "pay off" by refusing to let go of my negative self-image.

Step 6:   I have free will and can choose to adopt a positive self-image.

Step 7:   Even though I have been seeing myself as untalented, incompetent, and unworthy, the fact is that I do have abilities and can consider myself worthy.

Step 8:   God has given me the right to enjoy the world.

Step 9:   I was created with a mission, and I am working toward fulfillment of that mission.

Step 10: I have come to realize what I am, who I am, and why I am: I am a special creation by God, an imperfect being that strives toward perfection but never attains it. My mission is to become that which God intended me to be. My value lies not in perfection, but in trying to overcome the imperfections inherent in every human being. My efforts to become the best person I can be merit my having high self-esteem.

By working on these steps, you can then invoke divine help in overcoming the destructive death instinct and clear the window through which you will see your true self.

3

LOVING OTHERS

In our pursuit of proper living, Torah identifies the unconscious drives that can compromise our judgment and alerts
us to the effects those drives—our instincts for good and
evil—can have on our identity and self-esteem. But as
Maimonides says, "By virtue of nature, people seek to form
communities" (*Guide for the Perplexed*, 3.49). We seek out
relationships because we need other people in our lives. Our
actions are the foundation of those relationships, and only
through Torah's insistence on mutual respect will those bonds
be sustained.

I was deeply influenced by my father's attitude of seeing
the good in every person. He would frequently quote from the
prayer of Chassidic master Rabbi Elimelech of Lizensk, who
prayed, "Help me to see the good in every person and not their
faults." My father was also guided in his actions by Torah literature, which teaches, "The human being is dear, because
people were created in the likeness of God. God showed people special love by informing people that they were created in

the likeness of God, as it is written, 'For in the likeness of God did God make people' (Genesis 9:6)" (*Pirkei Avot* [Ethics of Our Fathers] 3:18). In this line of thinking, respect for another human being is on par with respect for God. Maimonides said, "Do not treat respect of others lightly, because preservation of human dignity may override rabbinical ordinances" (*Mishneh Torah*, Laws of Sanhedrin 24:10).

On the subject of loving and respecting the wicked, the Torah instructs that we must condemn and despise wickedness, while maintaining love and respect for the person. Granted, this is a most delicate and sensitive distinction, and admittedly not easily achieved. The Baal Shem Tov said, "I wish I had the love for the most righteous person that God has for the most wicked person."

Finding Diamonds

> Rabbi Eliezer said, "Let your friend's honor be
> as precious to you as your own."
> PIRKEI AVOT (ETHICS OF OUR FATHERS) 2:15

The Talmudic emphasis on respecting everyone enabled me to relate respectfully to many alcoholics and drug addicts who were social outcasts. I believe that the success I achieved in treating these people is in no small measure due to their feeling that I genuinely respected them, and I helped them to respect themselves. My father's teaching to see the good in every person and not a person's faults greatly enforced this.

In 1992 I opened a small rehabilitation unit in Beersheba, Israel, for ex-convicts who had been imprisoned for drug-related crimes. When I spoke to the group about the importance of self-esteem in recovery, Avi interrupted me.

"How can you expect me to have self-esteem?" he said. "I am thirty-four years old, and sixteen of those thirty-four years have been spent in prisons. No one will give me a job, and when my family is told that I am soon to be released from prison, they go ballistic. I am a burden and an embarrassment to them. They'd rather I'd be dead. Where can I get self-esteem from?"

I said to Avi, "Have you ever passed a jewelry store and seen the beautiful, scintillating diamonds in the window? Do you have any idea what a diamond looks like when it is taken from the mine? Like a dirty piece of glass! Someone who did not know any better would throw it in the trash. But there is a maven who knows that this ore contains a gem and sends it to the processing plant, which eventually produces a beautiful, valuable diamond.

"There is no way anyone can put beauty into a dirty piece of glass. The beauty was there all the time, but for thousands of years, that diamond was lying in the ground, covered by layers of grime. What the processing plant does is remove the layers of grime to expose the diamond.

"I know nothing about diamonds, but I do know something about *neshamot* [souls]. You have a beautiful *neshamah* with you. For many years it has been covered with layers of grime. If you stay with us, we will expose it for you and others to see."

Avi remained for three months of treatment and several months in a halfway house, then found a job. One day, Annette, the administrator of the halfway house, received a call from a family. Their elderly mother died and left an apartment full of furniture that they would like to donate to the halfway house. Annette called Avi. "We have this donation of furniture," she said, "but I have no way of getting it here."

"No problem," Avi said. "I'll get a truck and bring it."

Two days later, Avi called Annette. "I'm at the apartment with a truck, but there's no use bringing the furniture. It's all old and dilapidated."

"I don't want to disappoint the family," Annette said. "Bring it over. Maybe we can salvage something."

Avi brought the furniture to the halfway house, which is on the third floor of a building, and carried it up the stairs. As he dragged up the sofa, an envelope containing 5,000 shekels, about $1,286, fell from the cushions! You must remember that in his earlier days, Avi would break into a house for 20 shekels. Now he had 5,000 shekels in his hands, and he was the only person in the world who knew of this money.

"Apply the rule of 'finders keepers'?" Avi must have thought to himself. No. Avi called Annette and told her. She told him to call the family because it was their mother's money. The family donated the money to the halfway house.

When I attended the *chanukat habayit* (housewarming) of the renovated halfway house, Annette told me the story about Avi, who was present. I said to Avi, "Do you remember our first meeting, when I told you that there was a diamond within you? Many people who never stole a dime would simply have kept the money. For you to report the money was the shine of the diamond within you."

A visitor to the halfway house in Tel Aviv can see a bronze plaque on the front door, which was donated by Avi. It reads:

Diamond Processing Plant

Torah has enabled me to see the diamond in every person.

Partnerships in God's Greater Glory

> And all the angels supported the weight of the
> heavenly work by joining one to another.
>
> *V'KHULAM M'KABLIM*

We have countless opportunities to express our capacity for compassion and respect for others every day in our relationships. In fact, every exchange with another human being is a test to some degree of decent behavior, goal sharing, and our abilities to give and receive graciously.

Marriage especially has a lot to teach us about what is important in human relationships. In the Jewish wedding ceremony, the marriage bond is sealed with the bridegroom's giving the bride a ring and saying, "You are hereby consecrated unto me according to the laws of Moses and Israel." With this formal statement, the couple is now husband and wife. The marriage ceremony continues with the chanting of several blessings, the first of which is "Blessed is God, who created everything for God's glory." Interesting, but what is its relevance to marriage?

This blessing is recited to tell the couple that while satisfying each other's needs is indeed important, it should not be the foundation of the marriage. Rather, both partners should make "bringing greater glory to God" their goal in life, and they should establish a family that will further this goal. *That* is the foundation of the relationship. In this way, any problems that occur do not weaken the foundation of the marriage, and when the foundation is firm, problems can more easily be solved.

The second blessing that is recited is "Blessed is God, who has created man." The couple should remember that a human being is a unique creature, much more than *Homo sapiens*, an intellectual animal. Whereas all animals are self-centered (except for pets that may adopt human traits), a human being must be able to give of him- or herself and make sacrifices for the welfare of the other person. The relationship of marriage must be one of giving, rather than only receiving.

The passion for each other that generally precedes marriage tends to diminish with the passage of time, and unless the principles contained in these two blessings are operative, the bond may weaken and break. Marriages where each partner is willing to make personal sacrifices for the other partner can endure.

Allow me to share a personal anecdote with you. My father gained a fairly extensive knowledge of medicine as a result of visiting hospitalized patients every day and discussing their cases with their physicians. When he developed cancer of the pancreas with metastases to the liver, he said to me, "Chemotherapy does not do anything for cancer of the pancreas, does it?" I told him that was true. "So, undergoing chemotherapy will cause some very nasty side effects but will not prolong my life, right?" I told him that was correct. "Then we agree that there is no point in chemotherapy." I had to agree.

Meanwhile, the doctor told my mother, "There is not much we can do for the rabbi. Perhaps we can get three more months with chemotherapy."

"Three months?" my mother asked. "Why, for even three days one must do it." She told my father that he must undergo chemotherapy.

My father said to me, "I'm sorry that the doctor gave Mother wrong information. Chemotherapy will not extend my life. However, if I refuse chemotherapy, then when I die, Mother will say, 'If only I had insisted on chemotherapy, he would still be alive,' and she will feel guilty for not doing so. I don't want Mother to feel guilty, so I will take the chemotherapy.

"There are many things I did for Mother in the past fifty-two years. This gives me the chance to do one last thing."

Bringing greater glory to God and giving of ourselves: these two guiding principles of marriage can lead us in all of our relationships, helping to bring out the best in others as well as the best in ourselves.

Accepting Help Graciously

> A person should acknowledge and return a favor to someone who showed him kindness.
>
> SEFER HACHINUCH, MITZVAH 33

The comedian and my good friend Danny Thomas once said, "Success in life has nothing to do with what you gain in life or accomplish for yourself. It's what you do for others." This is true. As we have established, giving is one of the building blocks of lasting relationships. It is equally true that accepting the help of others is a sacred act, to express gratitude for others' kindnesses. But much like giving, accepting help is not always easy.

French author and seventeenth-century nobleman François Duc de la Rochefoucauld (1630–80) said, "Everybody takes pleasure in returning small obligations; some go so far as to acknowledge moderate ones. But there is hardly anyone who does not repay great favors with ingratitude."

My grandfather, a wise rabbi, echoed the same sentiment: "I know why that man dislikes me, and why that other person opposes me. But him? Why does he dislike me? I never did him any favors!"

Accepting the help of others and expressing gratitude isn't always difficult. Someone opens the door for you, and you say, "Thank you." You drop something and someone picks it up for you, and you say, "Thank you." The waiter serves your meal, and although you will pay for it and leave a tip, you say, "Thank you." It's common for people to acknowledge small kindnesses or favors and thank their benefactors.

But more significant favors can incite the opposite: ingratitude. Why should this be? What causes a person not only to be ungrateful but even to reject, alienate, and provoke the person offering help?

The Talmud sheds some light on this question. It relates that Moses chastised the Israelites, "You are ingrates, the children of an ingrate" (*Avodah Zarah* 5a). Moses was referring to Adam, who, when reprimanded by God for eating from the Tree of Knowledge, said, "The woman whom You gave me, she gave me the fruit of the tree" (Genesis 3:12). God had given Adam a beautiful mate, yet he turned around and faulted God, projecting the blame for his own disobedience on Eve.

In what way were the Israelites ingrates? For that, we must look at the Torah account of the Revelation at Sinai, when, upon hearing the voice of God, the Israelites said to Moses, "Hearing the voice of God is too awesome for us. You listen to God and convey God's words to us" (Exodus 20:16). God was pleased with their reaction and said, "Who can assure that this heart should remain theirs, to fear Me and observe My commandments all the days?" (Deuteronomy 5:26). Moses said to the Israelites, "This was your opportunity! When God said, 'Who can assure that this heart should remain theirs?' you should have said to God, 'You can assure it. You can implant within us the awe and reverence for You that would prevent us from deviating from Your commandments'" (Deuteronomy 5:26).

Very well. The Israelites were remiss. But in what way were they ingrates?

The *Tosafot* commentary on this exchange explains that the Israelites did not want to ask God for anything because they did not wish to be beholden to God. Accepting the gift of reverence would have obligated them to God as a benefactor, and they did not wish to feel obligated (*Avodah Zarah* 5a). The Israelites showed ingratitude in their denial of God's gift. (Note that the Talmud states that this occurred in the thirteenth century BCE. That means the essence of la Rochefoucauld's seventeenth-century statement was known to Moses three thousand years earlier!)

One reason for this dynamic is low self-esteem, the ubiquitous condition we discussed earlier. If you have low self-esteem, you may have great difficulty accepting favors and expressing gratitude because needing or receiving help from anyone can trigger feelings of inadequacy. This may be so distressing that you may deny that you received the favor at all. If you suffer from extremely low self-esteem, the discomfort may be severe. As a result, you may develop hostile feelings toward the person extending the offering, seeing the actions of the giver as the cause of your discomfort. I know an excellent physician who used to spend eighteen hours a day in the hospital or office and only six hours at home. He knew that he was competent as a physician and was, therefore, comfortable in the hospital or office. However, he did not feel that he had anything to offer *as a person*; he felt inadequate as a husband and father. As a result, he avoided home.

You are unlikely to have dependency feelings aroused by the service of a waiter or by someone holding the door open. These favors are small and transient and therefore are not a threat to your ego. However, when you cannot do things for yourself and require the help of other people in more significant, lasting ways, your unwarranted low self-esteem kicks in to reject any feelings of dependency. As an extreme example, a world-famous surgeon suffered a heart attack, and on the third day in the coronary-care unit, he removed the intravenous tube, detached the heart monitor, and walked out. His ego was such that he had to have others depend on him. For him to need help from others was anathema.

As the seventeenth-century poet John Donne expressed, "No [person] is an island." It is virtually impossible to go through life without the help of others; in some cases, it is downright foolhardy. Accepting the help of others is an expression of gratitude that celebrates our humanness. The Torah emphasizes the importance of gratitude in the ritual of "the first ripened fruits" (Deuteronomy 26:1–11), in which a person brings the first produce of his or her fields and orchard to the sanctuary and recites a lavish expression of gratitude. This was a most colorful and joyful ceremony and imbued the expression of gratitude with joy rather than possible indifference or resentment. This ritual began on the festival of Shavuot, and although Jews today celebrate this festival in commemoration of the momentous event of receiving the Torah, the Torah itself makes no mention of this, rather referring to the Festival of Weeks as *Yom Habikurim*, the day of bringing the first-ripened fruits (Numbers 28:26).

The Torah gives acknowledgment of gratitude greater importance than receiving the Torah! Why? Because the Midrash says, "Proper behavior is a prerequisite for Torah," and acknowledgment of gratitude is fundamental to decent behavior and lasting relationships.

The Supremacy of Action

> Treat no one lightly and think nothing is useless, for everyone has a moment and everything has a place.
>
> PIRKEI AVOT (ETHICS OF OUR FATHERS) 4:3

Can a person be ordered to have proper intentions? Can emotions be legislated? Can a person be commanded to show gratitude, to love someone, or not to envy someone? Love and envy are emotions that are elicited by relationship to an object and are not subject to being produced at will. How then can the Torah command such things as "You shall love God" (Deuteronomy 6:5) or "Do not covet your neighbor's possessions" (Exodus 20:14)?

We generally assume that intentions, or affects, are not something that we can produce at will. If, say, a woman does not like a certain coworker, she cannot simply decide, "I must force myself to like her." Yet the Torah dictates, "Love your fellow as yourself" (Leviticus 19:18). Just generating any level of love seems impossible, let alone loving someone as you love yourself. True, Hillel interpreted this verse for a proselyte as meaning, "Do not do to others what you would not want done to you" (Babylonian Talmud, *Shabbat* 31a). However, the manifest meaning of the verse seems to be an imperative to love another person.

The fourteenth-century scholar Rabbi Aharon Halevi, in his work *Chinuch*, provides us a solution saying, "Affect is determined by deeds." In other words, you *can* generate love for another person by acting in the way you would if you indeed loved that person. This principle may go all the way back to Sinai. The Torah states that when the Israelites were informed that God wished to give them the Torah, they declared, "We will do and we will listen" (Exodus 24:7). They put action first. (The Torah thus anticipated Dale Carnegie's classic *How to Win Friends and Influence People* by three thousand years!) In the Talmud this principle is applied to Torah study when it states that a person should study Torah even in absence of the desired intention (*kavvanah*) because the student going through the motions will eventually have the proper intention (*Pesahim* 50b).

Maimonides argued that a person can also use this principle of action to attain love of God. He explained that a person can arrive at love of God through the action of contemplating the marvelous works of God's creation. Indeed, if you appreciate the intricacies of the human body, you stand in utter awe of its Creator. For example, the brain is comprised of one hundred billion cells, all interconnected in the most marvelous fashion. Just think of this. The movements of each eye are brought about by the action of six muscles, which operate together to move the eye to the desired position. The six muscles of the right eye and those of the left eye must be perfectly coordinated, otherwise the person would have double vision. This coordination occurs via multiple nerve pathways in the brain. My professor of neurophysiology said that from the time the pitcher throws the ball until the batter swings at it, many thousands of neural transmissions occur. Even all the computers in the world combined could not approach the function of the brain! The marvel of creation, both the macrocosm and microcosm, testifies to the grandeur of God and leads not only to reverence, but also to adoration of God.

Similarly, a physician specializing in infertility said, "I was peering through the microscope at a fertilized ovum. I realized that henceforth, this single microscopic cell will be provided only with the elements carbon, nitrogen, oxygen, and hydrogen, and out of them it will manufacture a marvelous organism, a human being. At that moment I realized that there is a God."

So while Maimonides shows us that action can result in the proper intention, Abraham ibn Ezra, one of the most distinguished men of letters and writers of the Middle Ages, flips it around, showing us that by having the proper intention, we will naturally take the proper action—or inaction, in some cases. Take the tenth commandment, "You shall not covet" (Exodus 20:14). Abraham ibn Ezra says that a person will not have a desire for anything that is absolutely beyond his or her reach. Thus, if astronomers were to discover that a distant star is composed of diamonds, even the most money-hungry person would not give it a second thought. Stars are light-years distant, and inasmuch as a light-year is 5,865,696,000,000 miles, a person cannot even fantasize traversing that distance. Since the diamonds are totally beyond reach, no one would even desire them. Similarly, says Abraham ibn Ezra, if a person is sincerely and totally committed to the three previous commandments—"You shall not murder; you shall not commit adultery; you shall not steal" (Exodus 20:13)—there will be no possibility of acquiring another person's possessions; they are absolutely unobtainable. Essentially, "You shall not covet" is not, in fact, a commandment. Rather, it is a natural conclusion. If the previous three commandments are observed, then you *will not covet*.

Mandating affect through action works because the natural state of all matter is *inertia*. There is a fascinating midrash that states that over every blade of grass there stands an angel who whips it and commands, "Grow!" The grass seed has the water and the essential nutrients that enable it to grow. Why must it be ordered to grow? The answer is because the natural state of all matter is inertia, and without a force that compels it to grow, the seed would do nothing.

Indolence is the natural state of the human being. A person must be motivated to overcome it. This is expressed beautifully in Proverbs:

> I passed by the field of a lazy man,
> And by the vineyard of a man devoid of under-
>   standing
> And I saw everything coming up in thistles;
> The surface was covered with thorns
> And the stone wall was torn down.
> This I saw and set my heart to it
> I saw it and learnt the lesson:
> Yet a little sleep, a little slumber
> A little folding of the hands to rest,
> And your poverty will stalk you;
> Your want will come as an armed man.
>
> PROVERBS 24:30–34

We have biological and psychological drives that can overcome inertia, but in absence of such drives, we would do nothing. This is why we may lack motivation to do something we are told to do, even though we may know that it is the right and proper action to take. The motivation we have may not be sufficient to overcome our natural inertia. However, if we are determined to act even in the absence of any strong desire to do so and we force ourselves to do so, we overcome the inertia.

Once the inertia is overcome, the motivation that it is the right and proper thing to do kicks in. Thus, the attitude "Fake it till you make it" is not hypocritical.

In *Strive for Truth*, Rabbi Eliyahu Dessler, an influential Orthodox rabbi, Talmudic scholar, and Jewish philosopher, expands upon this principle, saying that it is indeed possible to generate love for another person by doing something for him or her. He says that the common belief that "you give to those whom you love" is fallacious. The reverse is true: "You love those to whom you give." If you find yourself disliking someone, do something nice for him or her. Affect follows action.

4

DEFENDING AGAINST OUR DEFENSES

If you see an object flying toward your head, you reflexively raise your hand to deflect it. Why? Won't your hand get hurt by it? Yes, but the danger of damage to your head is greater than damage to your hand.

Just when did you make that judgment? You didn't even have time to think about what defensive action to take. It is a natural physical response that your mind makes automatically.

That's the way our system operates. We take defensive actions without thinking about them. It happens automatically. But sometimes the body's defensive maneuvers may be counterproductive, as when it responds to a joint inflammation by forming scar tissue. It is the scar tissue rather than the inflammation that causes the deformity of arthritis. Similarly, our psychological unconscious defensive mechanisms may be damaging to our spiritual well-being.

Defending What Is Real—Or Is It?

> Every way of a man is rightful in his own
> eyes, but God examines the heart.
>
> PROVERBS 21:2

When Jerry was laid off in the recession, his father-in-law took him into his business. He could not give him a great salary, but at least it was something. At about the same time, Jerry's daughter had been accepted at a college. He had always dreamed she would attend college and was desperate to come up with the tuition. He reasoned that just as Stacy was his daughter, she was his father-in-law's granddaughter, and certainly he would want to help her just as he had helped Jerry. Jerry used this line of thinking to justify taking five thousand dollars from the business, with plans that he would return it later. Jerry's thinking was faulty, but the stress of having to provide for Stacy's tuition made him think that this was a "loan" rather than embezzlement.

Jerry's actions can best be identified as a defense mechanism described by Sigmund Freud as *rationalization*, which is essentially giving logical but false reasons for an act instead of true reasons. Rationalization is not making excuses. Excuses are conscious efforts to defend particular acts or failure to act. Rationalization is an unconscious process; the person truly believes his or her reasoning is correct. Thus, rationalization is self-deceptive.

A much earlier and graphic description of the self-deception of rationalization can be found in the Book of Proverbs, traditionally seen as authored by King Solomon in the ninth century BCE:

> The lazy man says: "There is a jackal in the way,
>   a lion in the streets."
> The door is already turning on its hinges, and
>   the sluggard is still on his bed.
> The sluggard already puts his hand on the plate,
>   but is too lazy to bring it to his mouth.
> The lazy man is wiser in his own eyes than seven
>   sensible counselors.
>
> PROVERBS 26:13–16

As this verse indicates, not only does the indolent person believe his reasons for inaction to be true, he cannot be convinced of their falseness even by seven wise counselors.

The Path of the Just (*Mesilat Yesharim*, 1740), a basic book of Torah ethics by Italian rabbi and philosopher Moshe Chaim Luzzatto (1707–46), elaborates on rationalization. Referring to people who are lax in their Torah observance, Luzzatto says, "Their *yetzer ra* [evil inclination] seduces them, and they would not be affected by this seduction were it not that they do not wish to see the truth" (*Mesilat Yesharim*, chapter 3). And again, "An indolent person can give you many excuses for his inaction and can quote authorities to support his position. He cannot see that he has distorted the words of the authorities, because his indolence makes him oblivious to his errors" (*Mesilat Yesharim*, chapter 4).

A person may rationalize actions or behaviors to justify refusal to change bad behavior. Martha, a nineteen-year-old college sophomore, decided to drop out of school. She spent her days hanging around with friends, smoking marijuana, staying up late at night, and sleeping the day away. She justified her behavior by saying, "I'm nineteen, it's my time to have fun. On my twenty-third birthday I'll deal with whatever I have to. I'll still have plenty of time." The rationalization makes her oblivious to the words of those who try to make her see the danger of these self-destructive ways. Gaining insight would necessitate making a change, and personal inertia does not permit this.

My father, an intuitive therapist, had his own story, based on a folktale, to demonstrate the phenomenon of rationalization:

When the first locomotive was introduced in Europe, word about this amazing phenomenon came to a small village. When the villagers heard that there was a wagon that moves without horses attached to it, they howled with laughter. "How stupid can people be to believe that a wagon will move without horses!"

When the stories about the locomotive kept on coming, the villagers decided that they must debunk this myth by a personal investigation. They chose the most enlightened person in the village to go to the big city and see what makes people believe that a wagon can move without horses.

The representative returned and called a town meeting. "My friends," he said, "it is not a fantasy. It is true." He was greeted by a derisive booing. When this subsided, he said, "Let me explain."

He then drew on the board a diagram of the steam engine, showing how the fire turned the water to steam, which pushed up against a piston that was connected to wheels. Each time the steam pressure pushed against the piston, that caused the wheels to turn and the wagon to move.

A few of the villagers promptly understood, but many were bewildered. The representative then laboriously explained, with many diagrams, precisely how the steam engine worked. One by one, the villagers came around. There was only one stalwart who shouted at them, "Are all you people as crazy as the city people? For thousands of years, wagons never moved without horses, and now you believe there is some kind of magic that moves wagons without horses! We sent this man to the city, and the city people must have hypnotized him to believe in this fantasy, and you are foolish enough to go along with it!"

By this time the villagers had come around to understanding how the steam engine works, so they all ganged up on this man, each one demonstrating convincingly how steam pressure can push a piston that turns the wheels. After a long discussion, the stalwart finally said, "Oh! Now I see. Of course, the steam pushes the piston, and it turns the wheels. How simple!"

Everyone breathed a sigh of relief. The representative then addressed the group. "Does anyone have any further questions?"

The stalwart raised his hand. "I understand everything perfectly: the steam pressure, the piston, the wheels. It's all very clear. I have only one question: on the diagram you made of that wagon, just where do you hitch up the horses?"

Inasmuch as rationalization is an unconscious process, it seems that we are at the mercy of our psyche's defensive maneuvers. What, then, can we do to avoid self-deception?

A simple, one-line guide to proper living is "Never defend a mistake." Lying to another person is, of course, sinful. It is robbing them of the truth. With rationalization, you are simply robbing the truth from yourself.

Mirror, Mirror ...

> The Baal Shem Tov said, "The world is a mirror. Inasmuch as a person is blind to one's own faults, God arranged it to see them in other people. The defects you see in others are your own."
>
> OHEV YISRAEL, LIKUTIM

As we've seen, in rationalization you deceive yourself into believing that what you did was right. But sometimes that doesn't work because the mistake is so obvious that you cannot justify it. The mind then has recourse to another defensive maneuver: "Okay, it was a mistake, but it was not my fault. It was someone else's fault."

Charles Schulz portrays this in his inimitable way in his *Peanuts* cartoon strip. Peppermint Patty, who never studies or does her homework, phones Charlie Brown.

"I failed again, Chuck, and it's all your fault," Patty says.

"My fault?" Charlie Brown asks.

"I need someone to blame," Patty says.

Accepting responsibility for failing would mean that she has to study and do homework, which she detests doing. The way to obviate what she detests is placing the blame on someone else. "Charlie Brown didn't study or do his homework, which is why I failed." Blaming Charlie Brown makes no sense, but blaming does not have to make sense. It is a defensive maneuver to make life easier.

As we have seen, the natural state of all matter is inertia, and it takes effort to change something from its natural state. People who are loathe to exert such effort simply blame someone or something else, and this absolves them from making any effort.

We begin this behavior in childhood. "I didn't do it. It was Jimmy." Or, "He hit me first." As we grow older, our blame shifting becomes more sophisticated. Everyone is to blame for the economic recession: greedy bankers, CEOs, stock manipulators. By blaming them we can look away from our own irresponsible lifestyle of buying everything we desire even when we cannot afford it and bankrupting ourselves by assuming impossible debts. "I drink because my wife nags me. Get her to stop nagging me, and I won't drink." Make *her* change. Marriage counselors describe a most tragic form of shifting blame in the case of the husband who batters his wife and says, "See what you made me do?!"

The propensity to blame is very deep-seated and can overwhelm logic. The Torah relates that Jacob's wife, Rachel, was childless, while her sister Leah, Jacob's other wife, had many children. In exasperation, Rachel said to Jacob, "Give me children—otherwise I am dead!" (Genesis 30:1). When Rachel was ultimately blessed with a child, she said, "God has taken away my disgrace" (30:23). What disgrace was she referring to? The Talmud says that Rachel said, "Now, if anything goes wrong, I can blame the child. If Jacob says, 'Who broke the dish?' or 'Who ate all the figs?' I can say, 'Your son did it'" (Genesis 30:23, Rashi).

I sincerely doubt that Rachel harbored so foolish a thought. Rather, this is the Torah's way of telling us how powerful is the tendency to blame. It is a profound psychological insight and alerts us to be on our guard. It is easy to blame, but blaming is counterproductive.

Sigmund Freud labeled this psychological defense mechanism *projection*, and it was later elaborated on by Freud's daughter, Anna, who was also a psychoanalyst. Simply defined, "projection" is a psychological defense whereby a person perceives in others the motives he or she denies having personally. Thus, the cheat is sure that everyone else is dishonest.

But the Talmud preempted Freud by two thousand years, saying that the defects a person sees in others are the person's own defects (*Kiddushin* 70a). This was codified into law by Maimonides, who ruled that if a person accuses another person of being of illegitimate birth, he should be suspected of being of illegitimate birth himself (*Mishneh Torah*, Laws of Forbidden Relationships 19:17).

It is related that the Baal Shem Tov once saw a person violate the Sabbath. He concluded that he must have somehow violated the Sabbath himself, else he would not have noticed it. Although he could not recollect doing so, he did penance and prayed for forgiveness.

Similarly, Rabbi Menachem Mendel of Lubavitch (1789–1868), third Chassidic leader of Chabad Lubavitch, was receiving his Chassidim when he abruptly told his aide not to admit anyone. He remained secluded for several hours, then resumed receiving his followers.

When asked about this self-imposed isolation, Rabbi Menachem Mendel explained, "When a person comes to me asking for advice on how to improve on a character defect, I know that he is a messenger from God to alert me to that character defect in myself. When I discover it, I can think of what I must do to eliminate it.

"The last person I saw told me about something wrong he had done, and try as I might, I could not find a trace of that in myself. But knowing what the Baal Shem Tov said, I realized that I must be in denial of that defect in myself. I, therefore, prayed the *Tehillim* [Psalms] until I was able to detect that defect in myself."

You may challenge this idea, saying "Why must I conclude that if I see a fault in others that I, too, have that fault?

Suppose I just happened to see someone doing something wrong. Why is that a reflection on me?"

A simple experiment clarifies this. Have ten people stand on a busy street corner for several minutes, and then ask each person to describe what he or she saw. It is very likely that you will get different answers. One person saw one thing, another saw something else; yet all ten people were exposed to the same scene. What made one person notice one thing and another person notice something else? You may say, "She just happened to see this, and the other person happened to see something else." Freud would never accept this, because for him, there are no "just happens." If two people are exposed to the same objects and yet they differ in what they saw, it is because each one was drawn to what he or she saw. Drawn by what? It can only be by a psychological need to see that object rather than another.

Understanding projection can help you identify your character flaws and allow you the opportunity to correct them. But it can also provide you with the impetus to exercise your positive character traits by turning projection on its head. The Talmud says, "Who is a wise person? One who can learn from every person" (*Pirkei Avot* [Ethics of Our Fathers] 4:1). When we see other people doing good deeds, we should emulate them. If we see them doing something wrong, we should do a thorough self-search to discover our own shortcomings.

Not Seeing What Is There

> There is essentially no difference between a physical blindness and a self-induced psychological blindness; that is, closing one's eyes to reality.
>
> *PATH OF THE JUST*, CHAPTER 2

But what if we don't want to acknowledge our shortcomings? We are familiar with the concept of visual hallucinations. A person in a toxic delirium may see things that do not exist. There is a flip side to this phenomenon, which is *not* seeing something that does exist.

When I was an intern in medicine, I had a patient who had undergone surgery for removal of a malignant tumor. Jane knew that she had cancer. She was given chemotherapy intravenously, treatment that often involved several needle punctures each time because it was difficult to find a vein. One time, I was asked to administer the medication. I found a vein on the back of her hand that I was able to enter with a small needle on the first try. From that day on, Jane insisted that I be the only one to give her the medication.

Jane came in for treatment every Sunday, when she knew I was on duty. She spoke freely about having cancer and how fortunate she was to be living at a time when medicine had developed a treatment for the illness.

After several months, however, the chemotherapy was no longer effective, and Jane was admitted to the hospital with shortness of breath and joint pains. She was very angry, saying, "I don't know what it is with you doctors. I've been coming here regularly and no one has been able to find what's wrong with me."

I was stymied. She knew she had cancer and had referred to it many times. How could she say that no one had found what was wrong with her?

What Jane was experiencing is known as "denial," a psychological term referring to the phenomenon that a person may be confronted with reality, yet deny what is obvious to everyone else. Essentially, denial is a psychological defense mechanism to protect a person from knowledge that would be too painful for him or her to tolerate. In Jane's case, as long as she felt well, "cancer" was an abstract term and was not threatening to her. When the disease began causing symptoms, she was so threatened by the awareness of what it meant that her mind just blocked the thought completely. She was no longer conscious of having cancer because she could not afford to be. Jane wasn't lying; lying is a willful distortion of the truth. Denial means that you are not aware of the truth.

We all know people in denial, those who are totally oblivious of something that is apparent to everyone else. Telling them the facts makes no impression. Their ears are essentially deaf to this information.

Examples of denial abound in scripture. The Book of Joshua relates that when Joshua conquered Jericho, he razed the city and pronounced a curse on anyone who would attempt to rebuild it, that all that person's children would die (Joshua 6:26). Years later, Chiel of Beth-El, although he knew of Joshua's curse, began rebuilding Jericho, and his oldest child died. As the rebuilding went on, his children continued to die, until the youngest died when the gates of the city were erected (1 Kings 16:34). Rabbi Chaim Shmuelevitz points out that Chiel was in denial. He knew of the curse, he saw his children dying, but Chiel did not associate the two.

In Genesis 18, we read that an angel told Sarah she would bear a child at age ninety. "Sarah laughed at herself, saying 'After I have withered shall I again have delicate skin?' God asked Abraham, 'Why is it that Sarah laughed…. Is anything beyond God?'" Abraham chastised Sarah for her lack of faith in God, and "Sarah denied it, saying, 'I did not laugh' because she was frightened" (Genesis 18:12–15).

The apparent meaning is that Sarah lied. But Rabbi Yitzchak Meir of Gur said that the matriarch Sarah was too spiritual a person to lie. He translates the last verse not as "Sarah denied it," but rather that "Sarah was *in denial.*" Sarah could not believe that she could have questioned the word of God. That was unthinkable! When she said, "I did not laugh," she was telling what she believed to be the truth.

The phenomenon of denial is especially important in character development. You may not be aware of thoughts and feelings whose awareness would be extremely uncomfortable or threatening to you, and therefore you cannot address them.

Rabbi Yehudah Leib Chasman (1869–1936), one of the foremost *mussar* scholars and former dean of Hebron Yeshiva, expounds on denial by citing the encounter of Moses and Aaron with Pharaoh. Aaron cast down his staff, which turned into a snake. Pharaoh had his sorcerers perform the same miracle. Aaron's staff then returned to being a staff, and as a staff, it swallowed the sorcerers' staffs. Pharaoh saw that Moses's and Aaron's powers were superior to his sorcerers' but was not impressed. When Egypt was smitten by the plague of frogs, Pharaoh begged Moses to remove the plague. He did not ask his sorcerers to do so because he knew they were powerless, yet because his sorcerers were also able to evoke frogs, he denied Moses's unique powers as an emissary of God. Even when his sorcerers, at the plague of lice, admitted their powerlessness, Pharaoh stubbornly refused to acknowledge Moses's superiority (Exodus 7:8–8:11).

Eventually, Pharaoh's suffering was so severe that he capitulated: "Your God is righteous, and I and my people are wicked" (Exodus 9:27), but this submission was short-lived. Pharaoh again became defiant.

Having treated many alcoholic people, this pattern of admitting and recanting is completely familiar to me. The alcoholic person gets into trouble because of his or her drinking and swears off alcohol. The commitment to abstain may last for hours, days, and even weeks, but rarely longer. An alcoholic has such a strong drive to drink, the misery and commitment are soon forgotten. I had a patient who suffered from severe pancreatitis as a result of his drinking, and the pain was so intense that it was not relieved even by strong narcotics. He writhed in pain for several days, tearfully swearing that he would never again touch a drop of alcohol. Three weeks later, he was drunk.

For the alcoholic person, the need to drink results in denial. With other people, there are different reasons. Pharaoh's was his ego, thinking himself to be a god: "The river is mine and I fashioned myself" (Ezekiel 29:3). Pharaoh could not accept that there was a power greater than his. Whatever the need may be, denial can render a person completely oblivious to reality.

Another example of denial: The Torah relates not only how Joseph saved Egypt from famine, but also that he turned over ownership of all the land of Egypt to the crown. In addition, he enriched Pharaoh's coffers by selling grain to all the neighboring countries that had been struck by famine (Genesis 47:14). After Joseph's death, "there arose a new king over Egypt who did not know Joseph" (Exodus 1:8). The Talmud says that he indeed *did* know Joseph, but that "he made himself *as if he did not know Joseph*" (Sotah 11a). In other words, the new king was *in denial* of Joseph.

The meaning here is not that he did know Joseph but acted as if he did not. The Torah clearly states that he did not know Joseph. This new Pharaoh did not have the slightest awareness of Joseph. It was as if Joseph, who saved the country from devastating famine and enriched the royal treasury beyond measure, had never existed.

The things we tend to deny are often our shortcomings and character defects that we wish to disown. If someone points them out to us, we may resist accepting reproof, and our psychological defensive apparatus may make us oblivious of them, thereby depriving us of the opportunity to correct them and grow spiritually. The Torah teaches us the phenomenon of denial because if we are aware of it, we may avoid reflexively denying our shortcomings, and be willing to look at ourselves more honestly.

Uncovering the Truth Behind Grandiosity

> What does God seek from you: only the performance of justice, the love of kindness, and walking humbly with your God.
>
> MICAH 6:8

We have all encountered a "know-it-all" sometime in our lives. You know the person—the guy who thinks he can never do wrong, the woman who has all the answers; if there are problems, they were most certainly caused by somebody else. This is the narcissistic personality, and one of its greatest dangers is that, because the narcissist can do no wrong, the personality disorder prevents us from recognizing the trait within ourselves.

The term "narcissist" is derived from the Greek myth of Narcissus, a handsome young man who fell in love with himself when he saw his image reflected in the water. The narcissist is self-centered and motivated by nothing other than selfish drives. If you are a narcissist, you expect everyone to pay homage to you. You are easily angered when your wishes are frustrated, and you are likely to demand absolute obedience from everyone you know, particularly your loved ones. Control freaks and spouse abusers are invariably narcissists.

As a narcissist, you never think there is anything wrong with you, so you do not consult a therapist. The therapist will be consulted by a family member, often a spouse or a child, who complains of the impossibility of living with you.

In actuality, the term "narcissism" is a misnomer. As a narcissist, you do *not* love yourself at all. To the contrary, you feel grossly inadequate and utterly worthless, and you react defensively to these distressing feelings of *despising* yourself by thinking yourself to be the greatest. You desperately need your feelings of superiority to be confirmed by others, which is why you demand adoration. Trying to deflate your feelings of grandiosity only causes you to intensify them because this touches at the source of your pathology. This defensive grandiosity may progress to paranoia.

This theory was confirmed by the thirteenth-century scholar Rabbi Yonah of Gerondi, who wrote, "The vain person, feeling his utter emptiness, tries to denigrate others in order to be able to feel superior to them" (*Rabenu Yonah al Hatorah*, p. 53).

Dealing with a narcissist is difficult because the person cannot see that he or she has character defects. The grandiosity borders on delusion, which, by definition, is refractory to logical argument. You cannot simply tell a narcissist, "Stop thinking that you're the greatest."

We can find some guidance, however, in the writings of the Jewish ethicists. The first step is to address the narcissist's self-awareness, to recognize character strengths and personality assets. This gets to the root of the vanity, as Rabbi Yonah has pointed out. Second, the ethical writings instruct the narcissist to *act* in a humble manner, to avoid ostentatious clothes, to speak softly, to look up to others, to avoid denigrating anyone, to avoid seeking acclaim or being seated in a place of honor. According to Rabbi Aharon Halevi's principle, "affect is determined by deeds," that we discussed earlier, acting in a humble manner will lead to feeling humble.

This principle is evident in a letter from philosopher and biblical commentator Ramban (Moses ben Nachman, 1194–1270) to his son, Nachman. There is no evidence that Nachman was in particular need of discipline, and the letter is one of inspiration that has been widely printed in prayer books as well as in pamphlet form.

Ramban begins his letter by instructing his son to avoid rage, pointing out the detrimental effects of rage as stated in the Talmud (*Nedarim* 22a). He goes on to say that avoiding rage will lead to humility, which is the finest of all character traits.

The obvious question: If humility is the finest of all character traits, why did Ramban not tell his son simply to work on becoming humble? The answer is that if Ramban felt his son lacked humility, it would be futile to tell him to become humble. That would be a direct assault on his vanity and, as with the narcissist, would be counterproductive. Ramban, therefore, did an "end run," instructing his son to control his rage. This is not as threatening to a narcissist, because controlling rage is compatible with grandiosity. Ramban's technique is a brilliant psychological maneuver.

Based on the assumption that narcissism is a desperate attempt to escape feelings of unworthiness, the antidote to narcissism is to eliminate the intense self-deprecation that is its underlying cause. This self-deprecation is often the result of a person's being unable to accept the drives and impulses that are inherent in a human being and leads to a person's disowning part of him- or herself.

The ethical writings state that there is one aspect of vanity, a narcissistic trait, that is constructive, and that is for a person to feel that he or she must abstain from certain acts because they are beneath his or her dignity. I recall that as a child, when my father disapproved of something I did, he would say, "That doesn't become you." He disciplined me by telling me I was too good, rather than saying that I was bad, thus helping me develop a positive self-image.

It is possible that by studying the Chassidic and *mussar* works, a narcissist may break through the delusional grandiosity and gain some insight into the reality of his or her character. The emphasis on humility does not cast an aspersion that a person is a narcissist, but rather that there are normal, inherent traits that a person should overcome. Uprooting feelings of vanity, and identifying them, are the first steps.

Fooled by Anger

> A person who is in wrath, if he is wise, he loses his wisdom; if he is a prophet, he loses his prophesy.
>
> BABYLONIAN TALMUD, *PESAHIM* 66B

We've addressed the common but often more complex defense mechanisms of rationalization, projection, denial, and narcissism; often these are unconscious reactions of which we are not aware. But what about something as seemingly simple as anger, which is a conscious, physical reaction? Perhaps it is not as simple as we think.

A great deal of psychotherapeutic time and effort is directed toward helping people cope with anger, and some serious errors have been made regarding anger management. For instance, it is a common belief that "ventilating" anger or acting it out by hitting a punching bag or the like helps relieve anger. But in his excellent book *Make Anger Your Ally*, clinical psychologist Dr. Neil Warren says, "More importantly, the overwhelming majority of psychological research on anger expression makes it clear that aggressive behavior facilitates more aggressive behavior rather than less" (p. 31). This recent research confirms the statement in the Talmud, "A person in rage achieves nothing but rage" (*Kiddushin* 41a).

There is some confusion in Torah literature regarding anger management because the Hebrew word *kaas* is applied to three distinct phases of anger: (1) the feeling of anger when provoked; (2) the acting out of anger; and (3) the retention of anger (and/or resentment). To clarify things, I will use the term "anger" to refer to the feeling aroused by provocation, "rage" to refer to the acting out of anger, and "resentment" to refer to the retention of anger. Thus, Maimonides' oft-quoted statement that anger is a sin as grave as idolatry is a mistranslation. Maimonides is codifying the statement of the Talmud that "one who breaks things in anger is equivalent to an idolater" (*Shabbat* 105b). Clearly, Maimonides is referring to rage rather than to the feeling of anger.

The Talmud spares no words in condemning rage:

> When a person is in rage, all the forces of hell overwhelm him. (*Nedarim* 22a)

> When a wise person is in rage, his wisdom leaves him. (*Pesahim* 66b)

> When a person is in rage, he does not even consider God. (*Nedarim* 22b)

> The life of one who is constantly angry is not much of a life. (*Pesahim* 113b)

The Talmud notes that on three occasions Moses was in rage, and all three times he erred. The first instance occurred on the day the Sanctuary was inaugurated, when two sons of the high priest, Aaron, died because they brought an unauthorized offering. Moses told Aaron that the mourning should not relieve him of partaking of the inaugural offerings. When Moses found that one offering was destroyed rather than eaten, he became angry and reprimanded Aaron. He later admitted that he was in error (Leviticus 10:16–20). The second instance happened when the Israelites attacked the Midianites who had seduced some of the Israelites to licentiousness and idolatry. Moses was angry that they spared the women who had been the seductresses. Moses then forgot the laws of how to "kosher" the utensils taken in the spoils (Numbers 31:13–24). The third instance occurred when the Israelites demanded water. Moses was angry for their lack of trust in God and berated them. When God instructed him to command the rock to issue water, Moses beat the rock instead of speaking to it (Numbers 20:10–13).

The toxicity of rage is stressed in the scriptures, especially in the Book of Proverbs:

> An irascible man stirs up strife, and a man of wrath commits much transgression. (29:22)

> Do not associate with a man of temper. And do not approach a man of wrath, lest you learn his ways and bring danger to your soul. (22:24–25)

> Rage is cruel and wrath is overwhelming, and who can withstand jealous rage! (27:4)

In dealing with rage, Dr. Warren suggests that it is important to anticipate the possibility of being provoked and preparing yourself for it in advance, to subvert the "automatic" response that is likely to occur when initially provoked. Natural instincts are not typically in line with traditional anti-outburst techniques, such as counting to ten or taking a moment to reason that the provocateur may have acted out of stress. Dr. Warren is essentially instructing us to train for moments when we will be provoked to anger, much like airplane pilots train in advance to know what to do if trouble arises. They cannot wait to reach for the instruction book when trouble occurs. Their training involves practicing on simulators, anticipating possible emergencies. This enabled Capt. Chesley Sullenberger to make a textbook-perfect landing of his disabled jetliner on the Hudson River in New York City in 2009, saving the lives of the passengers and possible victims of a ground landing.

The Talmud states that Rabbi Akiva would pray each morning for divine help in avoiding rage. Rabbi Chaim of Volozhin (c. 1750), ethicist and Talmudist, would pray daily: "Master of the Universe! I know that I will be exposed to the danger of sin, and particularly to anger. Please protect me from rage." This is an excellent technique to prepare yourself for such an eventuality.

The Talmud relates a charming story about the great Sage Hillel, who had a reputation of being averse to rage:

A man wagered four hundred *zuzim* (Babylonian silver coin) that he could provoke Hillel. One Friday afternoon, when Hillel was washing for Shabbat, he stood in front of his house exclaiming, "Anyone by the name of Hillel here?" Hillel wrapped a sheet about himself and went out. "Yes, my child, I am Hillel. What can I do for you?"

"I have a question," the man said. "Why are the heads of Babylonians spherical?

"That is a fine question," Hillel said. "It is because they do not have competent midwives."

A bit later, the man returned. "Anyone by the name of Hillel here?" he said. Again Hillel said, "Yes, my child, I am Hillel. What can I do for you?"

"I have a question," the man said. "Why do the Tarmedians have watery eyes?"

"That is a fine question," Hillel said. "It is because they live in a sandy area, and the wind blows the sand into their eyes."

It was now getting close to Shabbat, and Hillel was making last-minute preparations, when the man returned. "Anyone by the name of Hillel here?" he said.

Hillel came out. "Yes, my child, I am Hillel. What can I do for you?"

"Why do the Africans have broad feet?"

"That is a fine question," Hillel said. "It is because they live in a swampy area, and that makes them more sure-footed."

The man said, "I still have more questions to ask, but I'm afraid you will get short with me." It was now almost Shabbat. Hillel sat down near him and said, "Ask whatever you wish."

"Are you the Hillel that is the Jewish leader?" the man said. "Yes," Hillel responded.

"Well," the man said, "I hope there are not many like you. I lost four hundred *zuzim* because of you."

Hillel said, "Perhaps you have learned something. It was worth losing even eight hundred *zuzim*, but to know that you cannot provoke me into rage." (*Shabbat* 30b)

Although you may not have control over experiencing anger when provoked, it is possible to subsequently divest yourself of the feeling. It isn't enough to avoid being provoked into expressing rage, as Hillel illustrates. You must let go of it internally as well. Holding onto unexpressed anger, also known as resentment, has negative long-term effects both physically and spiritually.

Dr. Warren cites evidence that "resentment is like acid in our bodies." Resentment elicits the physiologic "fight or flight" response, including increased heart rate, elevated blood pressure, discharge of glucose into the blood, shift of blood supply from the digestive organs to the muscles, and increased blood coagulability. Festering in the system with no legitimate way to be expressed, these changes can affect vital functions.

The early commentaries on the Talmud agree, saying, "Anger interferes with digestion" (*Shitta M'kubetzet, Nedarim* 22a). The psalmist says, "My eye is dimmed because of (retained) anger" (Psalm 6:8).

But as Solomon says in Ecclesiastes, "Anger lingers in the bosom of a fool" (7:9). Nursing a resentment allows someone whom you dislike to live inside your head without paying rent. That is indeed foolish.

Rejecting the Bribes of Our Desires

> For God created man *yashar* [upright, straightforward, honest], but man has sought many calculations.
>
> ECCLESIASTES 7:29

Every society has its rules of right and wrong. What would you be like if there were no such laws? Would you be just another beast, or would you have a sense of propriety?

The Talmud makes an interesting statement that gives us insight into the possible answer to these questions. "If the Torah had not been given, we would have been responsible to learn respect for private property from the observation of ants [if an ant has touched a speck of grain, no other ant will touch it], fidelity from pigeons [pigeons are monogamous], and decency from cats [that cover their excreta]" (*Eruvin* 100b). But why? If the Torah had not been given and we were to learn behavior from the observation of animals, perhaps we would have learned robbery from tigers, promiscuity from dogs, and vanity from peacocks. What would have obligated us to learn decent behavior?

I have been critical of the scientific classification of the human being as *Homo sapiens* because it seems to imply that *sapiens*, or intelligence, is *the* defining feature of the human being. If this is true, then the person with the highest intellect is the finest human being. We know that this is not so. Some very intelligent people have lived lives that are far from exemplary. Prior to World War II, the most advanced country in terms of intellectual achievement was Germany. Adolf Hitler was hardly the finest of humanity.

If the purpose of a human being's existence is contentment, to maximize self-gratification and self-centeredness, then the marvelous brain we have is counterproductive. Cows have a much more peaceful and contented life than do human beings. (Indeed, one dairy boasts that its milk is the finest because it comes from the most excellent cows. Its motto is "Milk from Contented Cows.") Anxiety, depression, and a host of other human miseries are the products of an intelligent brain. If self-gratification is the purpose of human existence, God would not have endowed the human being with so superior a mind. And if we do not subscribe to God's creating man and woman, we must admit that nature does not do anything so foolish. Animals' instincts and abilities are those needed for survival. Plato's philosophy, Shakespeare's plays, and Beethoven's symphonies are not essential for survival of the human species.

If the Torah had not been given, we would have been expected to realize that our enormous mind was not intended for mere self-gratification and that if we were meant to have the traits of tigers, dogs, and peacocks, we would not have been endowed with the human brain. Clearly, the human mind was intended to enable a person to master the more self-centered traits and to realize it was necessary to learn restraint from ants, pigeons, and cats.

"God created man *yashar*, but man has sought many calculations." These calculations are the rationalizations we use to justify self-gratification. If we use our *sapiens* wisely, we will realize that we differ from animals in many ways, over and above simple intellect.

Thomas Jefferson, third president of the United States, in the Declaration of Independence said that man's inalienable rights are "life, liberty and the pursuit of happiness." But we also have duties as well as rights, and among these duties is the pursuit of truth. The ability to search for truth is one of the features that distinguishes humans from other living things.

The Torah forbids a judge from accepting a bribe, because "a bribe will blind the eyes of the wise and distort the words of the righteous" (Deuteronomy 16:19). Regardless of how wise and pious a person may be, a bribe renders a person unable to be objective and see the truth. Regardless of how much a person may try to be objective, a bribe will cause a person to favor the one who gave the bribe.

We are all "bribed" by our desires. If we deliberate whether or not to do something, our judgment will invariably be slanted in favor of what we desire. A person is presented with a business deal that is perfectly legal and not frankly dishonest, but there are some ethical concerns. The desire for the profit it may produce may cause him or her to rationalize and dismiss the ethical issues. A woman has an intense desire for an attractive man and is told by everyone that he is an opportunist who will exploit her. Her passion for him blinds her to the risks in the relationship.

You were created in the likeness of God. God is true and *yashar* (Deuteronomy 32:4). You, then, share the same traits of honesty and straightforwardness. But you also have physical drives that may conflict with this inborn sense of propriety and may distort your ability to apply it. Given that we all have desires that crave gratification, how can we hope to ever be objective?

Rabbi Yisrael of Rhizin (1798–1851), one of the foremost Chassidic leaders in Poland, concluded that we should be aware that we are constantly being bribed. We have drives that we wish to gratify, and the desire for gratifying these drives will cause us to think in a way that will enable the gratification.

"Observe a tightrope walker," Rabbi Yisrael said. "The way he maintains his balance is that when he feels himself being pulled to one side, he over-corrects by leaning a bit toward the opposite side.

"Whenever you are considering whether or not to do something, think about which way would be most pleasing to you. Then think of as many reasons as you can why you should not do it. That way, you will be neutralizing the 'bribe' that would cause you to justify whatever it is that you'd rather do."

5

ADAPTING TO ADVERSITY

At some point in your life, you will be confronted with adversity—we all are, it is inescapable. Adversity can affect you physically, such as by natural disaster or disease, or mentally, such as by a significant loss or emotional upheaval. You may experience economic adversity, which can significantly affect your lifestyle—you may lose your job due to company downsizing or have your personal retirement savings wiped out in a company bankruptcy. Adapting to adversity can be difficult and distressing, and though we cannot control what happens to us—avoiding adversity altogether—Torah gives us guidance on various ways that we can control how we react.

Finding a Sense of Purpose and Self-Value

> What is [human]kind's obligation in this world?
>
> *PATH OF THE JUST*, CHAPTER 1

As a society, we generally value something for one of two reasons: it is *functional* or it is *ornamental*. If you have a beautiful grandfather clock that can no longer tell time, you keep it because it is a handsome piece of furniture. On the other hand, if a can opener is dull and can no longer open cans, you discard it. With its function gone and having no aesthetic feature, it is worthless.

For you to have a sense of purpose, you must see yourself as either ornamental or functional. There are indeed some very handsome people who may consider themselves to be ornamental, but even this value wanes with advancing age. Most people cannot claim to be ornamental, hence their value must lie in their function, and that function can be a sustaining source when faced with adversity.

According to a midrash, King Solomon was thrown off his throne by Ashmidai, king of the demons, leaving him homeless and destitute. In an act of survival, Solomon went begging from door-to-door for food, introducing himself by saying, "I am the king." People jeered at him as a madman. How could a person who has resorted to begging think he is royalty? But Solomon knew the truth. He was king, and he had faith that he would eventually be restored to his throne.

The Talmud says that initially Solomon was king over a vast empire. When he was thrown off his throne and had to beg for food, he was "king only over his walking stick" (*Sanhedrin* 20b). Rabbi Chaim Shmuelevitz says that in the depth of his impoverishment, Solomon was still "king over his walking stick," that is, he never forgot that he was king. His circumstances were disastrous, but he did not allow them to crush him. He maintained his sense of royalty and function even when he had to beg for food.

"A person must be most cautious when he suffers a fall, that he should not allow the fall to harm him even more than the actual adverse circumstances," Rabbi Shmuelevitz said. "If he will strengthen himself even in his decline and maintain his personal value under all circumstances, there is hope that he will rise and return to his former status and even higher than that."

But just what is the function that can give a person enduring value? We live in a culture that worships at the altar of productivity. Whether or not we wish to admit it, we often value people according to how much we feel they contribute to society. People who are unproductive, whether due to advanced age or infirmity, may lose a sense of worthiness. This is in no small measure responsible for depression in the elderly or even in, say, middle-aged parents who experience the "empty nest syndrome" and feel relatively useless when all their children leave home and they do not have to tend to their needs. Workers who lose their jobs may feel depressed not only because of curtailed income but also because they have been rendered unproductive.

I found myself up against the challenge of productivity when I was asked to make a house call on a young woman who was profoundly depressed. Ruthie was suffering from a fulminating form of multiple sclerosis that had completely paralyzed her and rendered her blind. She was totally bedfast and could not care for her personal needs. She could not see or touch her two children. She asked me, "Why am I alive? I am of no use to anyone. I am just a burden to everyone. Why doesn't God let me die?"

I did not know what to say. People who linger in a coma do not present the same problem. We sustain life even when there is little hope of recovery. But these people generally do not suffer, and they do not challenge us with the questions this woman had. Ruthie was fully conscious, aware of her condition, and deeply depressed. Psychiatry, which trained me to treat depression as a disease, had not prepared me to deal with Ruthie's depression, which was founded in reality and could not be alleviated with antidepressant medications.

To have said something empathic like, "I can understand how you feel" seemed ridiculous. No one could understand Ruthie's feeling of utter uselessness. This was one of those situations where the only modicum of comfort I might provide came from my just being there, because the feeling of utter loneliness can be terrifying. I sat with her for a while and told her I would return the next day.

What happened next can only be providential. The following morning in the daily Talmud class, I came across this episode:

The great Sage Rabbi Eliezer fell seriously ill, and his students came to comfort him. One student said, "Our master! You are dearer to us than a father and mother. A father and mother can provide a child only with this world, but you, our master, have provided us with the World to Come." Rabbi Eliezer did not acknowledge this student's comment.

Another student said, "Our master! You are dearer to us than the sun. The sun can provide a person only with this world, but you, our master, have provided us with the World to Come." Rabbi Eliezer remained silent.

A third student said, "Our master! You are dearer to us than the rain. The rain can provide a person only with this world, but you, our master, have provided us with the World to Come." Again, Rabbi Eliezer remained silent.

Then Rabbi Akiva spoke up. "Suffering can be precious," he said. Rabbi Eliezer said, "Help me sit up so that I can better hear what my child, Akiva, has to say."

The other students had said things that should have comforted Rabbi Eliezer. Why did he ignore them and listen only to Rabbi Akiva?

Resting on your laurels is vanity and achieves nothing. Rabbi Eliezer valued life because it provided him with the opportunity to do God's will. But he was now weak and bedridden and could do nothing. This depressed him, and the fact that he had achieved much in the past did not comfort him in the least. He could be comforted only if there was something he could do now.

Rabbi Akiva implied that the divine will demands that we maximize ourselves spiritually. This is what human beings were created for, and doing so is self-fulfillment, which is the only thing that Rabbi Eliezer felt was of value. However, in his condition, he did not see what he could do that would be spiritually fulfilling.

Rabbi Akiva understood that self-fulfillment comes from a person's doing whatever he or she can do at any particular moment, given that person's condition at that moment. What Akiva told Rabbi Eliezer was, essentially, "When you had the ability to teach, your self-fulfillment was teaching. Your condition now does not permit you to do that or anything else that you consider important. All you can do now is accept your suffering with trust and faith in God, and when you do that, you are fulfilling yourself every bit as much as when you taught us."

I went back to visit Ruthie and shared with her this teaching of the Talmud.

"But I am angry at God for letting this happen to me," she said.

"That is perfectly understandable," I said. "The Talmud says that a person is not culpable for feeling angry at God when one is suffering. Your challenge now is to try to accept that God's judgment is fair and just and that we cannot possibly fathom God's infinite wisdom. Because that is all you can do now, that is as meritorious as all you did when you actively cared for your children and the household. If you wish, I will come back to help you work toward that goal, which is now your self-fulfillment."

Ruthie accepted my offer and thanked me. With the help of Torah I had helped her recalibrate her idea of what productivity is and, in so doing, reclaim her sense of purpose and worthiness.

Managing Grief

> After the death of Abraham, God blessed Isaac, his son.
>
> GENESIS 25:11

There are different forms of grief. In Ruthie's case, she was grieving the loss of her function, her sense of purpose. By taking steps to resolve her grief and begin healing, she was warding off one of the most difficult spiritual, emotional, and physical challenges that humans experience: unresolved grief. The Jewish tradition provides a framework for encouraging grief work in many cases of mourning, but not all. It is often the actions of others—sometimes merely being present—that help the afflicted through these times. The spiritual payoff for both parties can be immeasurable.

Unresolved grief may occur when a grief-stricken person is very depressed from a significant loss of some kind. Well-meaning relatives may get a doctor to prescribe a tranquilizer, often to alleviate their own discomfort of seeing a loved one in such pain rather than to soothe the person who suffered the loss. Anesthetized with tranquilizers, the grief-stricken person seems to behave "normally." But months or even years later, the person may develop severe emotional symptoms because the work of healing from grief was not done.

In his classic paper *Mourning and Melancholia*, Sigmund Freud describes a close interpersonal relationship as having "feelers" extending from one person to another. When the person toward whom these feelers are directed dies, the feelers are left dangling in midair. Grief work enables the survivor to gradually retrieve these feelers and essentially redirect love that was given to the other person back into the self, which can increase the survivor's self-love in a positive manner, or redirect it toward other family members. If the grief work is not done, these emotional extensions—the feelers—are not absorbed. They hang out there, leaving the grief-stricken person feeling raw, vulnerable, and susceptible to depression.

Obviously, grief work cannot be done unless the reality of the death is accepted. When the pain over the loss of a loved one is extremely severe, the mind may rely on defense mechanisms, such as denial, to relieve the pain. Although at a conscious level the person may know that the loved one has died, the unconscious mind, which often defies logic and reality, continues to believe that the person is still living. This delays the necessary grief work that will lead to healing.

Torah mandates grief work. Traditionally, close relatives—spouse, sibling, parent, child—must observe a week of mourning known as *shivah*, during which they may not work or go to school and are required to follow certain practices of mourning. Other family members and friends are expected to fulfill the mitzvah of visiting the bereaved and consoling them. Friends come to the home and share with the mourners their memories of the deceased. People bring food and otherwise take care of the mourners. The week of mourning helps the survivors accept the reality of their loss.

A lesser degree of mourning is prescribed for the next three weeks, during which time the mourners may not attend festive events. All the mourning rituals bring home the reality of the loss, thereby enabling the survivors to go on with normal life. When a parent dies, some mourning continues for a full year. During this time, the mourner recites the *Kaddish*, which is not, as some may think, a memorial prayer. Rather, the *Kaddish* praises God and expresses the hope for peace and universal recognition of God.[3]

While comforting the bereaved is indeed a mitzvah, we must use discretion in what we say. Sometimes it is better to say nothing at all. As the Talmud instructs, "Let the mourner take the lead" (*Moed Katan* 28b).

One of my most painful experiences as a rabbi was officiating at the funeral of a three-year-old child who wandered off from the summer home and drowned in a nearby lake. When I visited during the *shivah*, the room was full of family members and close friends. Gradually, they all left the room, leaving only Edith, the mother, and me.

---

3. The *Kaddish* is also recited on the *yahrzeit*, the anniversary date of the death according to the Jewish calendar (as well as at certain other prescribed times during the year). It is common to experience depression on the anniversary of a loved one's death. Commemorating the anniversary with prayer mitigates the severity of the anniversary reaction.

Edith began crying and expressing profound feelings of guilt and sadness. "Why didn't I run to the lake immediately when she was missing?" she cried.

The next day, the scene was repeated. Everyone left the room, and Edith cried to me. This repeated itself every day of the *shivah*. I said nothing, because I had nothing to say.

After the *shivah*, Edith's father called. "I want to thank you for all you did for Edith," he told me.

I was perplexed. I did not think I had done anything for her. Then I realized that all the people in the room who shared personally in her grief tried to divert Edith from the pain of her terrible loss, and she had no chance to ventilate her feelings. I just listened, and that was what she needed. Her grief work had begun.

Healing Body and Spirit

> A merry heart keeps the spirit up, but a depressed spirit desiccates the limbs.
>
> PROVERBS 17:22

While my experiences with Ruthie and Edith demonstrate that merely being present can provide the comfort necessary to begin to heal the spirit, there is also *scientific* research that shows the positive spirit of community can influence healing the body.

The idea that how a person thinks and feels can have a significant effect on the body is relatively new, first appearing in scientific circles in the early twentieth century with the work of the American physiologist Walter Cannon. Cannon was able to demonstrate that emotions such as rage and fear produce adaptive changes in the body, giving rise to the "fight or flight" reaction. When you feel threatened, for example, a number of bodily changes occur that enhance your ability to flee or to fight off the attacker. Subsequent studies by research psychologists greatly advanced this concept, and it became evident that even less intense emotions, such as chronic anxiety or low-level hostility, can result in physical damage.

It is of interest that historically the medical community was not very receptive of this. When I attended medical school in the late 1950s, for instance, virtually nothing was taught about psychosomatic medicine, the mind-body connection. To physicians, mind was mind, and body was body. Inasmuch as emotions cannot be measured in the laboratory, they were seen as unimportant in understanding the function of the physical human being. Although it was common practice to prescribe sedatives and tranquilizers for conditions such as high blood pressure and peptic ulcer, the theoretical basis for doing so was dismissed. It was not until later that medical education began to include psychosomatic concepts.

Unfortunately, the term "psychosomatic" was often misunderstood to mean that the problem was "all in your head," that is, the patient was seen as feigning symptoms. But nothing could be further from the truth. Psychosomatic diseases are real. A perforated ulcer or heart attack is not imagined, just as the stressful or emotional events that triggered them are not imagined. One of the mechanisms that confirms the basis for psychosomatic diseases has been discovered in recent years. The brain produces chemicals known as endorphins (endogenous morphine). Endorphins transmit neural messages among the brain cells, and they operate by attaching to endorphin receptors on other brain cells. More recently, it was discovered that there are endorphin receptors on the digestive tract. This, then, is the mechanism whereby brain activity—thoughts and feelings—

affect the digestive tract, resulting in various digestive disorders, such as peptic ulcer and irritable bowel syndrome.

Even more recently, it was discovered that there are endorphin receptors on T cells, the lymphatic cells that produce immune substances such as antibodies. This means that the immune system is under the influence of the mind!

While the medical community may be just catching on, the mind-body connection has been recognized in the spiritual community for thousands of years. For example, the traditional Jewish prayer for the sick is for "healing of the spirit and healing of the body" (*refuat hanefesh u'refuat haguf*). Not only is the need for healing the spirit recognized, but in the prayer it is given precedence to healing the body. This indicates that there cannot be effective physical healing unless there is spiritual healing. Also notable for spiritual healing is visiting the sick (*bikur cholim*), one of Judaism's foremost mitzvot, which guides us to bring comfort and support to the sick, and lift their spirits through the connection of community. The Talmud states that visiting a sick person relieves the patient of one-sixtieth of the illness!

The effects of both positive and negative emotions on the body were also noted by Solomon in the Book of Proverbs:

Deferred hope makes the heart sick. (13:12)

The light of the eyes rejoices the heart;
Good news gives marrow to the bones. (15:30)

The life of the flesh trains the heart,
But envy rots the bones. (14:30)

A man's spirit sustains him in sickness.
But if the spirit is broken, who shall uplift it?
(18:14)

I've seen the beneficial effect of an upbeat mood on health and healing firsthand. A forty-three-year-old man was devastated by the diagnosis of a malignant disease with a very grave prognosis. To help ease his suffering and heal his spirit, I helped him visualize joyful scenes, such as the celebrations and dancing at weddings, bar mitzvahs, or Simchat Torah. He was able to re-create these scenes in his mind to the point of hearing the music and feeling himself participating in the dancing. I instructed him to practice this and other happy-scene visualizations three times a day. When he survived long past the doctor's prediction, the doctor said, "I don't know what it is that you're doing, but do more of it." He is now active in business, more than thirty years after receiving his catastrophic diagnosis.

Healing the body by way of the spirit works. Make an agreement with a friend to e-mail him a joke every day, and in return, he should e-mail one to you. If you have already heard the joke, ask him to send you another one. It will help preserve your good health and his. In case of physical and mental illness, a belly laugh is good medicine.

Trusting Happiness

You shall not fear the terror of the night, nor of the arrow that flies by the day.

PSALM 91:5

It is beneficial to have friends to help lift your spirits, but it is also important that you be able to conjure an upbeat attitude on your own. This can be more difficult for some people who, for reasons unknown, always expect that something bad is going to happen. This is considered a form of anxiety known as morbid expectations. For example, they may interpret a ringing telephone as someone calling to report a tragedy. Inasmuch as the dreaded event is unknown or even recognized as a fantasy, there is nothing they can do to cope with it.

I must admit that I have been afflicted with morbid expectations. Years ago when I was practicing psychiatry, I had a general rule that I was not to be interrupted when seeing clients except in cases of emergency. The hospital operator knew this.

So when the phone rang during an interview, I answered it anxiously. When the operator said that it was my daughter-in-law, I froze, assuming something terrible had happened. Instead, my daughter-in-law cheerfully declared, "*Mazal tov!*" I had become a great-grandfather.

I knew that my grandson's wife was due to deliver any day. Yet I jumped to a negative conclusion rather than to a positive one.

We can counter morbid expectations by strengthening our faith in ourselves and our relationships with others and with God. There are countless stories in Jewish lore that illustrate the benefits of trust in God. For instance, Rabbi Moshe Alshich (1508–93), a prominent biblical commentator, delivered a sermon on Shabbat in which he said that a person's earnings are determined on Rosh Hashanah and that if people would have absolute trust in God, they would not have to work. Their *parnossah* (livelihood) would come to them.

Rabbi Moshe's sister was married to a very simple, pious man, who made a living as a porter, delivering merchandise with his horse and wagon. On Sunday, after returning from services and eating breakfast, the man took the Book of Psalms and began reciting the psalms leisurely.

"Why aren't you going out to work?" his wife said. "I don't have to work," the man said. "The rabbi said that God will provide for me."

"The rabbi did not mean for you to sit and do nothing," the wife said. "I am not doing nothing," the man said. "I am reciting the psalms."

The wife went to the rabbi's home. "My dear brother," she said, "you must be careful what you say in your sermons. My husband refuses to go to work. He says that God will provide for him."

"If he is really sincere in his trust in God," Rabbi Moshe said, "God will indeed provide for him."

Later that day, a man came to the door. He saw a horse and wagon near the house and asked if it was for hire. The husband lent him the horse and wagon.

This man was a highway robber, who had robbed and killed people. He had buried the loot and now wanted to retrieve it. He dug deeply for the loot and loaded it on the wagon. When he went into the pit to see if there was anything more, the walls of the pit caved in, burying him.

The horse remained standing there, but as time went on, the horse got hungry and, being familiar with the paths, found its way back to the house. The husband was enriched with the robbers' loot.

When Rabbi Moshe learned of this, he said, "It is not enough to just express trust in God. This man's trust was absolute. He believed wholeheartedly that God would provide for him, and his trust was so profound that he sincerely believed that he already had what God had predetermined for him. That is the kind of trust in God that works."

Similarly, the Baal Shem Tov, the founder of the Chassidic movement, was directed to a certain person who had achieved absolute trust in God. The Baal Shem Tov went to meet him and asked to stay with him for a few days so that he could learn from him.

The man told the Baal Shem Tov that he earned his livelihood by operating a flour mill, which he rented from the local *poritz* (feudal lord). The rental was a thousand rubles, and the due date was the next day. "Do you have the thousand rubles?" the Baal Shem Tov asked. "No," the man said. "I don't have even ten rubles." "Are you going to borrow the money?" "No," the man said. "There is no one I can borrow from." "Then how do you plan to pay the *poritz*?" the Baal Shem Tov asked. "That is God's problem, not mine," the man said. The Baal Shem Tov saw that the man was in a cheerful mood, going about his business as if he had not a single worry.

Later that day, a representative from the *poritz* came. "Do you have the rent money?" he asked. The man answered, "Why are you bothering me today? The rent is not due until tomorrow." "Very well," the representative said, "but just remember, the *poritz* does not deal kindly with tenants who do not pay the rent on time." "Go away," the man said.

The following day, the Baal Shem Tov asked, "How are you going to get a thousand rubles today?" The man answered, "I told you yesterday, that is God's worry, not mine."

At noontime, the *poritz*'s representative came to collect the rent. The man said, "I am not in arrears until the day is over. Don't bother me." The representative said, "You can expect a harsh reaction if you don't pay the rent. The *poritz* may have you flogged, destroy your house, or imprison you in the dungeon." The man did not appear worried.

That afternoon, three grain merchants came. "We want to buy the grain from all the *poritz*'s farms. We know that you have dealings with him, and we want to engage you to negotiate for us."

"I'll be glad to," the man said. "My fee is a thousand rubles."

"A thousand rubles?" the merchant said. "Have you gone mad? Fifty rubles is the most we will pay."

"Then go to the *poritz* yourself or buy the grain elsewhere," the man said. "My fee is a thousand rubles, nothing less."

The merchants left angrily. The Baal Shem Tov noticed that the man's cheerful disposition had not changed.

About an hour before sunset, the *poritz*'s representative came. "Now is your last chance to pay the rent," he said. The man said, "Come in and wait a while. It is still an hour to sunset."

A bit later the three merchants returned. "We've looked elsewhere to buy grain, but we found nothing. Here is a thousand rubles to negotiate for us with the *poritz*." The man took the money and said, "Come with me to the *poritz*," and invited the representative to join him.

The Baal Shem Tov said, "Now I know what it means to have trust in God."

There are also benefits in simply trusting in your own capacity to receive and experience happiness. When Maimonides was the court physician to the sultan of Egypt, he wrote to him, "It is just as likely for good things to happen as bad things. Why allow yourself to be tormented by expectations of grief when it is just as easy to anticipate joy?" (*Regimen Sanitatis*).

I have seen Maimonides' sentiment in action. At one meeting of Alcoholics Anonymous, a woman related the sordid tale of her years of drinking and using drugs, and her recovery in the program. She then shared the following story:

I am a rabid football fan. The New York Jets are my team. I never miss a game. One weekend, I had to be away, so I asked a friend to record the game on her VCR. When I returned, she handed me the tape and said, "By the way, the Jets won."

I started watching the tape. Horrors! The Jets were playing terribly, and at half-time they were twenty points behind. Under other circumstances, I would've been a nervous wreck, pacing and hitting the refrigerator. But I was perfectly calm, because I knew they were going to win.

Ever since I came into this program and made a decision to turn my will and life over to God, I know that in the end it will turn out all right. Sometimes I'm twenty points behind, but I know I'm going to win.

It is unclear why morbid expectations occur. Perhaps it is a case of adhering to the old adage "Prepare for the worst" so that you are not devastated by bad tidings. One way to avoid morbid expectations is to begin the day meditating and imagining a pleasant, joyous scene, which may set a positive tone for the day. I spend a few moments visualizing a childhood scene of being at a summer cottage with my days spent playing baseball, swimming, fishing, reading comic books, or doing other enjoyable things. It is a great way to start the day with an upbeat spirit.

Each day I also say Psalm 112, in which verse 7 asserts that with trust in God there is no reason to fear bad tidings. True, sincere trust in God is not easy to achieve. I say the psalm not as a statement about myself, but rather as a prayer: "Please help me develop trust in You, so that I will not anticipate bad tidings." There are many times that I have been twenty points behind, and I pray that God brings things to a favorable conclusion.

The Power in Hope

> Trust, because there is hope.
>
> JOB 11:18

With all of these approaches to coping with adversity, there is never any justification for despair. This is a fundamental principle of Torah. Rabbi Nachman of Breslov said, "There is no such thing in reality as despair. A person who feels hopeless is delusional. Despair simply does not exist" (*Likutey Moharan*).

The Torah relates that Abraham's castoff concubine, Hagar, was wandering in the desert with her son, Ishmael, and they ran out of water. She left Ishmael under a tree and sat far away because she could not watch Ishmael die. An angel appeared to her and told her that Ishmael would live. "Then God opened her eyes and she saw a well of water" (Genesis 21:14–19). There was no miraculous creation of a well. The well was always there, but in her despair, she did not see it.

That is what may happen when a person loses hope. There may be a solution to your problem, but in a state of despair, you cannot see it. One of the reasons psychotherapy is effective is because in a state of hopelessness, the therapist enables you to see the solution, thus helping you regain hope.

The psalmist says, "Hope unto God, be strong and strengthen your heart, and hope unto God" (Psalm 27:14). Why the repetition? Because you may have to gather strength to be able to hope. If you find that you cannot hope, you must try to strengthen yourself so that you will be able to hope, whether that hope is for you or for others. As Mark Twain said, "You can't pray a lie." Nor can you convince someone of something that you don't believe yourself.

During World War II, a family that belonged to my father's congregation was notified that their son was missing in action in Europe. Understandably, they were devastated. My father tried to lift their spirits by telling them that their son was probably a prisoner of war and would return when the war ended. Once a week, my father would visit the family to keep up their hopes that their son was alive.

When the war was over, it was found that, indeed, their son had been a prisoner of war. When the son returned to his base before returning home, he found a stack of letters that my father had written to him. These were written before each weekly visit to the parents' home. My father had to reinforce his own hope that the son was alive, in order to be effective in conveying hope to the parents.

It is no coincidence that the motto of Gateway Rehabilitation Center, the facility that I established for the treatment of alcoholism and drug addiction, is "Where hope has a home." Many people whose lives lay in shambles as a result of their addiction feel hopeless and beyond recovery. I have never lost hope for even the most deteriorated addict. I believe that my feeling conveys itself to them and that this glimmer of hope gives them the courage to try to rebuild their lives.

When a person is poor and has no money for food, you give or lend that person some money of your own. It is no different with hope. If a person has no hope, you give that person some hope of your own. Perhaps this is what the scripture meant, "Those who hope in God exchange strength" (Isaiah 40:31).

One Day at a Time

> The God-fearing man lives in terms of days, and the lawless one in terms of years; yet even years are not sufficient to bring him the fulfillment of his schemes.
> RABBI SAMSON RAPHAEL HIRSCH, *THE WISDOM OF MISHLE*, P. 25

Hope is essential to adapting to adversity. But the reality is that it can be difficult to sustain over the long haul. Whether you are summoning hope for yourself as you struggle with a long illness or sharing hope with a friend grieving the loss of a loved one, the psychic and spiritual energy it requires to hold on to hope long-term can be a challenge in itself.

In 1935, a rather significant event occurred that can help us sustain hope. Two alcoholics, helping each other in trying to stay sober, began to offer their help to other alcoholics. The results of their efforts came to be known as Alcoholics Anonymous (AA), which now has many millions of members across the world. The success of AA led to the formation of twelve-step groups for other addictions, such as drugs, food, gambling, and sex.

Prior to AA, it was felt that alcoholics were hopeless. Medicine and psychiatry had nothing to offer them but the instruction of total abstinence for life. But Bill Wilson, the cofounder of AA, realized that if an alcoholic person was told that he/she could never drink again, he/she was sure to fail. To the alcoholic, liquor was the only thing that allowed him/her to function. Wilson, therefore, said that whereas giving up alcohol for life was so formidable a challenge that a person would not even give it a try, it was possible to avoid drinking for just that one day. The alcoholic was instructed not to think about tomorrow's drinking. "There is nothing you can do today about tomorrow's drinking. Leave that until tomorrow.

Just stay sober this one day." And so the philosophy of "one day at a time" was launched. This concept has enabled millions of people to recover from serious addictions.

How new was this concept? Rabbi Chaim of Chernovitz (1769–1815) writes in his commentary on Psalm 95:7:

> For God is our God and we can be the flock God pastures and the sheep in God's charge—even today, if we but heed God's call. The *yetzer ra* causes one to shun serving God, by saying, "Look how long you will have to suffer deprivation." The answer to this is "I only have to do so today." The following day, one says so again. This is what the psalmist meant, "Even today, if we but heed God's call." Just today.
>
> RABBI ELIEZER HALEVI HOROWITZ, *AMOROT TEHOROT*

This concept was not new for Rabbi Chaim either. The psalmist says, "Blessed be my Lord, day by day" (Psalm 68:20). We may even trace this back several thousand years earlier, to the manna in the desert: "I shall rain down for you food from heaven; let the people go out and pick *each day's portion on its day*" (Exodus 16:4).

I was reminded of a conversation with a friend who was in recovery with AA:

"You've been sober a long time, John, haven't you?" John just shrugged. "How long have you been sober?" I asked.

John took out a little calendar from his vest pocket, paged through and said, "9,482 days."

"What is that?" I asked. "Twenty years? Twenty-five years?"

John said, "I don't know, Doctor. Yesterday was 9,482 days. If I make it through today by the grace of God, then it will be 9,483 days. You can afford to think in terms of years. I can't."

John died at age eighty-four. The night before his death he wrote in his calendar, "16,312."

One-day-at-a-time has application far beyond recovery from addiction. Using such an approach is common in surmounting all kinds of adversity—from grief work to achieving personal and professional goals. The Torah relates that Jacob loved Laban's daughter Rachel and that he had to work for Laban seven years to win her hand in marriage. "So Jacob worked seven years for Rachel, and they seemed to him a few days because of his love for her" (Genesis 29:20). At first this makes little sense. To someone who must wait for his beloved, each day is a century! But a more careful reading shows that the verse should be translated, "and they seemed to him *like single* days." In other words, Jacob was able to tolerate seven long years because he took "one day at a time."

I too have used this approach. In my medical internship, I saw that I was going to be under the preceptorship of an impossible-to-please physician for the next year. I survived it by taking one day at a time.

Whatever the challenge is, whether it is an eight-year college course, a long recovery from a disabling illness, or surviving the loss of a loved one, we have the capacity to handle it if we bring it down to bite size. "I can do nothing today about tomorrow's challenge, so there is no point in taking it on. I can handle today."

One day at a time.

6

PERFECTING THE WORLD, PERFECTING OURSELVES

We hear a great deal about the need for repairing the world (*tikkun olam*), but we can only speak of repairing something if we know the function of the object. For example, if we do not know what a food processor is supposed to do, we would be hard-pressed to restore it to its proper function. To speak sensibly about *tikkun olam*, then, we must have a concept of the purpose of the world's existence.

If we do not assume an intentional creation, there is not much point in speaking of *tikkun olam*. If several billion years ago there was a spontaneous accident that resulted in energy being transformed into matter, which then underwent evolution until we had the world as it is today, then the world did not come into existence for any purpose, and there was no design or function for which it was formed.

This is reminiscent of the two loiterers who were brought before the judge on charges of vagrancy. The judge addressed the first loiterer. "What were you doing when the officer arrested you?" he asked.

"Nothing," the man answered.

The judge then asked the second loiterer, "And what were you doing when you were arrested?"

The second loiterer pointed to his friend and said, "I was helping him."

For there to be an ultimate purpose to the world, we must assume that there is a reason for its existence. There can be many intermediate purposes in a purposeless world, but no ultimate purpose. There is a purpose for filling my car's fuel tank with gasoline because that enables me to get to my office. But if I do nothing at the office, filling the gas tank to get there has little meaning. Similarly, if something is wrong with the car and I have it repaired, the repair has meaning only if I will then do something meaningful with the car. Repair of an automobile that will forever stand idle and never be put to any use is of no value. A purposeful world presupposes that it was brought into being for a reason.

True, creation of the world by God is a suprarational concept. If we understand God to be all perfect, then there is no reason for God to have created a world. An all-perfect being can have no need to do anything. You can have a desire and be motivated to do something. This desire or motivation indicates that you have some kind of lack, greater or lesser, and doing whatever you wish to do is intended to satisfy that lack. To say that God created the world for a reason (as we understand reason to mean) is not logical, because it would mean that God is happier with the existence of the world than without it. But that is an internal contradiction because it means that God is more perfect with an existing world than without one. However, an all-perfect being cannot become more perfect.

Noncreation of the world is just as illogical as creation because it assumes that something was always in existence, whether it was matter or energy. Our minds can grasp only those concepts with which we have had some sense experience, however remote it may be. "Eternity" and "infinity" are both nonrational ideas. We have no experience with anything that has no beginning and that is without end. Hence, a noncreated world that emerged from something that had no beginning can have no meaning.

With revelation, we have a starting point from which rational thinking can proceed. God informed us that God did indeed create the world, and our reasoning can proceed from there. It is much like the axioms upon which all geometry is based. To the believer, creation of the world by God is an axiom but remains an unsolvable mystery. Without revelation, we are adrift because there is no starting point.

According to Kabbalah, God "desired" to have a presence in a physical world. God's infinite majesty is well recognized in the celestial spheres, but for reasons known only to God, God "desired a dwelling place on earth." God's presence is everywhere, albeit concealed.

God wished to have a creature that can choose between right and wrong, good and evil. Neither animals nor angels can do this. Angels are pure spiritual beings and have no desires of their own. They cannot sin. Animals are pure physical beings, totally dominated by their biological drives. Animals cannot make choices because they must follow the dictates of their bodies. The human being, classified by science as *Homo sapiens*, is the only creature that has the ability to defy a bodily urge. We are endowed with a divine spirit that enables us to be moral and ethical beings, the crown of creation. When we live moral and ethical lives, we fulfill the purpose of our creation. Our manifestation of this unique, God-given ability to make moral and ethical choices gives God "a presence in the physical world."

If giving God a presence in the physical world is the purpose of creation, then a world that denies God this presence by unfettered hedonism, violating morality and ethics, is in disrepair. *Tikkun olam*, then, consists of bringing the world to a state where God's presence is manifested by people exercising their divine spirit. This brings God out of concealment.

The Chassidic master Rabbi Mendel of Romanov was walking with several of his disciples when they came across a child who was crying. Rabbi Mendel asked the child why she was crying, and she said, "We are playing hide-and-seek. I hid myself, but no one is coming to look for me." Rabbi Mendel turned to his disciples and said, "Can you imagine the agony of God, who concealed Himself in this world, but no one is looking for Him?"

The principle of *tikkun olam* is thus very simple: to fulfill the purpose of creation by behaving in a manner that will reveal the presence of God in the physical world. But while the principle is simple, its implementation is very difficult because it requires a person to subdue many urges that are innate to the animal component.

How is this to be brought about? The Talmud says that the phrase *v'ahavta et Hashem*, "you shall love God" (Deuteronomy 6:5), also means "you should make God beloved to others." This, the Talmud says, is achieved when a God-fearing person transacts honestly and speaks respectfully and pleasantly. People will then appreciate the beauty of devotion to God and will want to emulate those who love God.

The Talmud has an interesting approach to *tikkun olam*:

The world is judged according to the status of the majority of its population. If the majority of the people is meritorious, the world receives a favorable judgment. If the majority is sinful, the world receives an unfavorable judgment.

Each person is also judged according to the majority of his or her acts. If a person has more mitzvot [merits] than sins, the person is considered to be a *tzaddik* [righteous person]. If a person has more sins than mitzvot, the person is considered to be a *rasha* (bad person). Therefore, you should always think of the world as being composed of an exactly equal number of righteous people and bad people, and you should always think of yourself as having exactly the same number of mitzvot as sins. *The very next act you do will be decisive.* If the next act you perform is a mitzvah, you will have more mitzvot than sins, and this will tip your personal balance to the good side; you will be judged a *tzaddik*. The number of righteous people will now be greater than the number of bad people, and the world will receive a favorable judgment. If your next act is a sin, you will be judged a bad person, the number of bad people will be greater than the number of righteous people, and the world will receive an unfavorable judgment. (*Kiddushin* 40b)

The message of the Talmud is clear: repairing the world depends on you. If you wish to rectify the world, begin by rectifying yourself.

The Responsibility of Being Human

> The thing is very close to you, in your mouth
> and in your heart to observe it.
>
> DEUTERONOMY 30:14

As human beings, we have instincts for both good and evil, conscious and unconscious. To rectify ourselves—to live spiritually and properly—involves getting a handle on these impulses. Is this possible? Two hundred years ago, Rabbi Shneur Zalman made the revolutionary statement in the *Tanya* that "the mind can be master over the heart," meaning we can control things over which we think we have no control. He declared that this is an innate ability—every person has it. It is related that during Napoleon's invasion of Russia, Rabbi Shneur Zalman was suspected of siding with Russia. One of Napoleon's officers rushed in and placed his hand over Rabbi Shneur Zalman's heart, in the belief that if he was indeed in opposition to Napoleon, his heart would palpitate. When his heartbeat did not accelerate, it was assumed that the accusation was false.

This concept that "the mind can be master over the heart" was recently validated by biofeedback, a learned technique that enables a person to achieve voluntary control over bodily functions that were always considered to be involuntary. For example, people cannot ordinarily dilate or constrict their pupils at will. This is a reflex response to light and darkness. Yet with biofeedback training, a person can learn how to dilate the right pupil and constrict the left pupil simultaneously! The traditional teaching that there are two divisions of the central nervous system, the voluntary and involuntary, has now been replaced by the voluntary and less voluntary.

One of the common uses of biofeedback is the treatment of migraine headaches. The technique allows a person who suffers migraines to control the intracranial blood flow, thereby aborting a migraine attack. Biofeedback can also be used to eliminate muscle pain, reduce high blood pressure, restore bladder control, and mitigate epilepsy. This last task can be achieved by gaining voluntary control over brain waves.

This technique may not be as new as we might think. Some of our great Torah luminaries were able to devote themselves entirely to Torah study, getting along with a minimum of sleep. My great-grandfather, the *tzaddik* of Sanz, said, "A fast runner can cover a distance in one hour that takes others much longer. I am a fast sleeper, and I can achieve in one hour of sleep what may take others six hours."

This is by no means far-fetched. We now know that there are several phases of sleep. The REM (rapid eye movement) phase appears to be the effective segment of sleep. However, it may take forty-five minutes of non-REM sleep to achieve fifteen minutes of REM sleep. If a person could learn to control the brain waves so that he or she could enter the REM phase immediately, the person could indeed be a "fast sleeper."

The concept that "the mind can be master over the heart" has legal implications. For many decades, there was an admissible insanity defense of "irresistible impulse," according to which you could be judged "not guilty" of a criminal act if you were in so intense an emotional state that you could not control your actions—even if you clearly knew what you were doing and knew right from wrong. After the 1981 assassination attempt of President Reagan by John Hinkley, many states rejected the defense of irresistible impulse, but it is still applicable in some jurisdictions.

Torah categorically rejects the notion of irresistible impulse. The Talmud concurs, stating that a person is *always* responsible for his or her behavior (*Bava Kama* 26a). This applies to all stages of life.

In modern times, the concept of adolescence—a developmental stage between child and adult—has provided an acceptable period of irresponsibility. The parents cannot be held responsible because they cannot control their adolescent.

The adolescent is not held responsible because he or she is not yet a mature adult. Adolescents can literally get away with murder, and some do. This temporary "free pass" on responsibility is detrimental to society and could have lasting implications beyond the adolescent years because once a person has experienced several years of nonresponsibility, this ideation may linger long into adult life.

Torah does not acknowledge a status of adolescence and therefore grants no such free pass. Until age twelve if a female or thirteen if a male, a person is a child, and the parents are held responsible for their child's actions. At sunset on the last day of the eleventh or twelfth year, there is a momentous transformation: the child becomes an adult, and his or her actions on the day after are judged no differently than those of a forty-year-old person.

The words of the Talmud are true. *Adam mued l'olam*—a person is *always* responsible. That sense of responsibility is one of the foremost distinctions between human beings and other living creatures. It is unique to humankind, and diminishing the sense of responsibility is essentially diminishing a person's humanity.

Liberating Ourselves from Dependency

> That you may remember the day of your departure from Egypt all the days of your life.
>
> DEUTERONOMY 16:3

The mind may indeed be master over the heart, but under the pull of our evil inclination, that control can slip away from us before we know it. We are reminded of the antidote to this each year, when we are mandated to relive the Exodus from Egypt, thus replenishing our appreciation of freedom and the preciousness of all that it entails.

I know a man who came from a very Torah-observant home who fell into the trap of drug addiction. After he recovered, he attended his father's Passover seder, and when his father began reciting the Haggadah (story of the Exodus), "We were slaves ..." he interrupted him. "Father," he said, "can you truthfully say about yourself that you were a slave? You can say that our ancestors, thousands of years ago, were slaves. But you do not know what it feels like to be a slave and what it means to be free. *I* can tell you what it means to be enslaved. All the years that I was addicted to drugs, I was a slave. I did things that I never thought I was capable of doing, but I had no choice. The drugs were my master, and I had to do whatever they demanded. Today I am a free person."

Passover is termed "the festival of freedom," but it is not only referring to the enslavement by a tyrant several thousand years ago. True freedom involves our ability to choose to act in ways that encourage our spiritual well-being and the well-being of others. A person who loves life and knows that smoking can hasten her death, yet is unable to stop smoking, is as much a slave to nicotine as our ancestors were to Pharaoh. This is equally true of a person addicted to alcohol, drugs, food, sex, gambling, and yes, even to making money. When any improper behavior becomes compulsive and we continue doing it in spite of our awareness that it is destructive, we have lost our freedom.

Today we call this addiction, and we have many branches of modern behavioral and medical science dedicated to researching and treating it. But the illness and our knowledge of it isn't necessarily new. Over three hundred years ago there was a clear understanding of addiction and dependence.

Rabbi Moshe Chaim Luzzatto, author of *Path of the Just*, cites several statements in the Talmud that appear to conflict. On the one hand, the Talmud is critical of someone who abstains from permissible things: "Is it not enough for you the things that the Torah prohibits, that you wish to add new restrictions?" (Jerusalem Talmud, *Nedarim* 9), and "A person will have to give an accounting on Judgment Day for any permissible food that he saw, of which he did not eat" (Jerusalem Talmud, *Kedushin* 4). On the other hand, Nachmanides says that the commandment "You shall be holy" (Leviticus 19:2) means that a person should abstain from permissible things and that a Nazirite, who took a vow to abstain from wine, is considered holy, and so is a person who fasts (Babylonian Talmud, *Ta'anit* 11).

Luzzatto resolves this apparent conflict by saying that while we may indeed enjoy permissible things, we must take care not to become dependent on them. It is all too easy for "wants" to become "essential needs," and if that happens, we may deviate from proper behavior to procure them. We may see some things as optional, but if we become accustomed to them, they may become essentials, and we may lose our freedom whether or not to have them. We may do desperate things to obtain them, even resorting to self-destructive or antisocial acts.

People are vulnerable to becoming dependent on the tranquilizing effects of alcohol and drugs, the thrill of gambling, or the soothing effects of food. People may become dependent on making money far beyond their needs, and may engage in less than honest ventures in order to accumulate more. A person may become dependent on receiving acclaim and act ruthlessly toward anyone standing in the way. There is even addiction to people, when a person cannot free him- or herself from a destructive relationship.

After World War II, many survivors of the Holocaust came to Israel, some with nothing but the shirts on their backs. There was an appeal for used clothes, and people brought these to our congregation, where I bundled them and took them to the post office. One day, we received a letter thanking us for the clothes, and the letter was written on personalized stationery! I asked my father how someone who was dependent on charity could indulge in the luxury of personalized stationery? My father explained that this woman probably came from a very wealthy family. For her, personalized stationery was *not* a luxury. She took it for granted that this is something she must have, just as she must have food and shelter.

An additional understanding of addiction can be found in the writings of Rabbi Yehudah Leib Chasman. In the addiction field, we do not speak of an addict as having been cured. An alcoholic who has not had a drink for forty years is referred to as "recovering" rather than "recovered," because at any time, after forty years just as after forty days, relapse is possible. We speak of an addiction as being "arrested," which means that the possibility of relapse always exists, and a recovering addict must keep this in mind. If an addict believes he has been cured, he has a false sense of confidence, which in itself can result in relapse.

Any habitual behavior to which a person has become accustomed has the characteristics of addiction. Rabbi Yehudah Leib Chasman points out that when Moses sought to liberate the Israelites, their first reaction was: "Don't make waves." They had become inured to enslavement and to having their infants thrown into the Nile. But then they witnessed the awesome miracles of the plagues, and at the dividing of the Reed Sea they saw their cruel taskmasters dead. They were now free of them forever. Yet, when the Israelites were unhappy in the desert, they said to Moses, "We remember the fish we ate in Egypt, and the cucumbers, melons, leeks, onions, and garlic" (Numbers 11:5). They were longing for the "good old days" when they were brutally beaten and saw their children killed. A bit later, the Israelites rebelled and said, "Let us appoint a leader and let us return to Egypt!" (Numbers 14:4). The decades of enslavement had so habituated them to this lifestyle that, wretched as it was, they were desirous of returning to it. In essence, they were addicted to enslavement.

Regaining control once it has been lost is often very difficult, so the aphorism "an ounce of prevention is worth a pound of cure" holds true. We should be on the alert to avoid unhealthy dependencies. The message of Passover is that we should cherish our freedom, protect it forcefully, and refuse to surrender it to anyone or anything.

The Steps of Repentance

> I do not desire the death of the wicked,
> but that he repent his ways and live.
>
> EZEKIEL 33:11

But what happens when we slip, when we surrender to our evil inclination? Luckily, Torah anticipated this. In fact, the Talmud states that the concept of repentance predated creation. The commentaries say that God knew that people would be fallible, and before bringing people into existence, it was necessary to provide for their survival. Therefore, people were given the opportunity to correct their mistakes.

If we verbalize the nature of our wrongs, we may recognize them and take the necessary steps to rectify them. That is why Jews make a list of all our misdeeds and ask forgiveness each year on Yom Kippur, the Day of Atonement. But it makes no sense to ask to be forgiven for something if we plan to continue doing it. So we must do *teshuvah*, the sincere regret for having done wrong and the promise to ourselves not to repeat the wrong deeds.

Wrong deeds do not arise out of a vacuum. There is something within a person, some trait that enables a person to do wrong. These traits are character defects, which cause us to act in improper ways. In our quest for self-improvement and positive character development, we aim to identify and extirpate them. But if we find that they are innate to us, that because they are part of our biological makeup we cannot eliminate them, then we must ask God to rid us of them.

One of the most successful approaches to positive character development is drawn from the Twelve Steps of Alcoholics Anonymous. Though created to manage addiction to alcohol, and later rendered to address all kinds of addictive behavior, the Twelve Steps can be a spiritual practice of addressing our wrong deeds in general. Bill Wilson, the cofounder of AA, drafted the Twelve Steps in 1938, but a close look at the principles behind the steps will find roots in Torah and similarities to the practice of *teshuvah*.

Let me take a moment to explain that I specialize in treating addiction, but I didn't plan it that way. There was nothing in my medical school or even psychiatric training to interest me in addiction, and certainly little in my Torah studies—or so I thought. However, when I was urged by the Department of Psychiatry chief at the University of Pittsburgh to consider the director position at an acute psychiatric hospital, I reluctantly agreed to meet with Sister Adele, the facility's director.

I had spent two months' rotation in the three-hundred-bed psychiatric division of St. Francis, and I had no aspiration of undertaking a position of that nature. I explained to Sister Adele that I was not the man for the job—I wouldn't answer the phone on the Sabbath, I'd be taking my family to Israel for the summer (this was June), and I wouldn't return until October. But Sister Adele said, "We've waited this long, we'll wait longer." She escorted me to the hospital entrance and said, "I know you will come with us. The Holy Ghost sent you to us."

On October 1, I began a trial year as director of the St. Francis Department of Psychiatry and remained in that position for twenty years. Among the things I inherited was a thirty-bed alcohol detoxification unit, colloquially known as the "drunk tank." After two years of watching a revolving-door service—where the alcoholic person is admitted, stays until "dried out" and is then released, only to return on the next binge—I told Sister Adele that we needed a facility to address the next step, that is, rehabilitating an alcoholic person *after* having "dried out." Against insurmountable odds, we opened the Gateway Rehabilitation Center, a one-hundred-bed residential facility, in 1972. When the use of narcotics became widespread in the late 1970s, we began treating drug addiction as well as alcoholism, and I gradually became a specialist on addiction.

As I've mentioned previously, there are a number of addictions, the most common being alcohol, drugs, smoking, food, sex, and gambling. It seemed to me that traditional psychiatry was not effective in treating these and that the greatest success was found with the various twelve-step programs, all modeled after Alcoholics Anonymous, so I set out to learn more about the approach.

When I first began studying the Twelve Steps, I was surprised to find they sounded very familiar to me. The first two steps were: "We admitted that we were powerless over alcohol ..." and "Came to believe that a Power greater than ourselves could restore us to sanity." That struck a familiar chord. Of course! Talmud says, "A person's *yetzer* [instinctual drive] increases in strength each day, and if it were not for the help of God, one could not withstand it" (*Kiddushin* 30b). In 1938, Bill Wilson, the cofounder of AA, cited a principle that the Talmud had stated two thousand years earlier.

The familiarity continued with step three. Recognizing that following your own will had resulted in the debacle of alcoholism, when seeking recovery you are told that you must relinquish your own will and turn your life over to the care of God. That seemed to have been lifted from *Pirkei Avot* (Ethics of Our Fathers) 2:4, "Treat God's will as if it were your own will.... Nullify your will before God's will."

In step four, you must then do a " searching and fearless moral inventory," which is the *cheshbon hanefesh*, or the personal accounting, that the Chassidic and *mussar* writings demand of every person. I was indeed in home territory. Although medical school and psychiatric training had not prepared me to treat addiction, Torah study had apparently given me some valuable suggestions.

AA's steps five through nine focus us on rectifying wrongdoings. Regretting a misdeed and vowing to never do it again can be repentance for a wrong act that did not harm another person, but if you have harmed someone else, whether monetarily or emotionally, remorse alone is not enough. "I'm sorry I threw a rock at your window" does not undo a six-hundred-dollar repair bill. Torah requires that a person must compensate for the damage done and that God withholds forgiveness until restitution is made. If the harm done is not of a monetary nature, the transgressor must do everything possible to make amends. God does not forgive unless the aggrieved person has forgiven. This is another similarity between the Twelve Steps and what is prescribed in Torah.

In the morning prayer service we say that a person should be God-fearing and always admit the truth. The Torah does not condone coverups. It is the greatest mistake to defend a wrong act. So the tenth step of the Twelve Steps, which requires "when wrong, promptly admit it," is something right out of the prayer book (*siddur*).

The eleventh and twelfth steps draw on the spirituality advocated in the Torah literature of Chassidism and *mussar*, by speaking of improving conscious contact with God by "spiritual awakening." An addict is the prototype of a person who has surrendered freedom and is under the tyranny of the addiction. The spiritual awakening is the realization that it is beneath your dignity to be dominated by self-centeredness. This awakening enables a person to strive for the self-fulfillment of which a human being is capable.

The greatest indication that a person has risen above the animal level is the capacity to care for other people—giving time, energy, and possessions to help other people improve their lot in life. Torah refers to this as *chesed*, or acts of lovingkindness. This is rising above the animalistic self-centeredness and becoming "other"-centered. This is expressed in the second half of the twelfth step: "Having had a spiritual awakening as the result of these steps, we tried to carry this message to alcoholics, and to practice these principles in all our affairs." The latter phrase is a Torah requirement. The Talmud says,

"What small verse is the one upon which all of Torah depends? 'Know God in all your ways' (Proverbs 3:6)" (*Berachot* 63a). Torah rejects the dichotomy of "Give to God what is to God and to Caesar what is to Caesar." Nothing is out of the realm of "what is to God." We must be godly not only in prayer and in manifestly religious acts, but also in all mundane activities. We must transact spiritually, relate to people spiritually, eat spiritually, sleep spiritually, and think spiritually. Indeed, we must practice the principles of spirituality "in all our affairs."

As I began attending AA meetings, it became evident to me that the twelve-step program is not primarily an addiction recovery technique. Rather, it is a program directed toward helping you change your character for the better. This was concisely stated by a person on the twentieth anniversary of sobriety, who said, "The man I once was, drank. And the man I once was, will drink again." What the program had done was change him into a different, a better person who has no need to drink. This is why a program designed to help a person stop drinking can be equally effective for other self-defeating behaviors.

The Twelve Steps can help you break loose from personal enslavement of improper behavior by guiding you in the following:

Step 1: Acknowledging that you have become powerless over an undesirable behavior

Step 2: Realizing that only a power other than yourself can extricate you from this enslavement

Step 3: Making the decision to turn your will over to the Divine

Step 4: Carefully looking for your character defects and identifying them

Step 5: Admitting to God, yourself, and others the nature of your improper behavior

Step 6: Readying yourself to have the Divine remove your negative character traits

Step 7: Asking the Divine for help in eradicating them

Step 8: Identifying the people you harmed with your improper behavior

Step 9: Making amends with the people you harmed

Step 10: Continuing to take a personal inventory, and when negative traits reemerge, *promptly* admitting them

Step 11: Seeking to develop a closer relationship with God

Step 12: Having had a spiritual awakening as a result of these steps, making yourself available to help others

I have been attending meetings for the past forty-seven years and will continue to benefit from the program as long as I have character defects. Inasmuch as a human being can never reach perfection, I will continue to attend meetings as long as I live.

Bringing Along the Days

> And Abraham grew old, came with the days,
> and God blessed Abraham with all.
>
> GENESIS 24:1

Today we are blessed with a problem. How can a blessing be a problem? Modern medicine has extended life expectancy. Prior to the advent of antibiotics, wonder drugs, and modern surgery, the average life expectancy in the United States was forty. Today it is eighty! The doubling of life expectancy is certainly a blessing, but it has also created a problem for many elderly people who are no longer working and for whom life has become boring. Research has shown that the number of elderly people who regularly take tranquilizers is staggering. They numb themselves with drugs to tolerate being alive.

I once gave a demonstration of hypnosis in which I showed the phenomenon of hypnotic anesthesia. "I have a patient whom you must see," a surgeon said to me after the demonstration. "She is a wonderful woman who has done much for the community. She is very depressed. She is suffering from cancer and does not want to take narcotics to ease her pain because it dulls her thinking. She does not deserve to suffer, and you must help her."

Fran was brought to the office in a wheelchair. She could not enter more than a very light hypnotic trance, nowhere near the level for pain relief. In an effort to deepen the trance, I told her to allow her mind to go back to some enjoyable event in her life. After she emerged from the trance, she smiled and said, "That was really fun! Bill and I were out on a ranch, doing barrels." Fran explained that "doing barrels" was a maneuver in horseback riding. She and her husband frequently went out west and rode horseback.

In the next few sessions, I used the same technique. Fran reported reexperiencing cruises, whitewater rafting, and more horseback riding. Though Fran was clearly enjoying these remembrances, I was never able to accomplish pain relief. Thinking this was the best I could do for her, I taught Fran self-hypnosis, and three times a day she was to put herself in a trance and relive a pleasant experience.

I called the surgeon to report my inability to achieve pain relief, but before I had a chance to say a word, the surgeon said, "Dr. Twerski! Bill is so thrilled with what you are doing for Fran. She no longer uses a wheelchair, she goes around the house humming a tune, her appetite has improved, and she has gone back to church."

I was perplexed. What was I doing for Fran? I felt that I had failed to give her pain relief.

It eventually became clear to me. Most people live with an anticipation of good things that may occur in the future. Fran knew that she had no future and that her days were numbered. Although she could not hope to enjoy the future, she could enjoy the past. Hypnosis enabled her not only to recall pleasant experiences of the past that she had forgotten, but to actually relive them.

"It's so exciting!" Fran said. "When I get up in the morning, I can't wait to do a trance. I don't know what I'm going to recall." Fran died later that year. Bill said that she was happy to the very end.

Fran taught me a great deal. There comes a time in every person's life when we cannot expect much in the future. If we live our lives so that we can have many good memories of the past, we need not be bored or depressed.

The Torah tells us that "Abraham grew old, came with the days, and God blessed Abraham with all" (Genesis 24:1). The patriarch lived a spiritual life, and when he grew old, he was able to bring all his days with him, to recall and enjoy the past. That was indeed a divine blessing.

I doubt whether a person in the last days of life has ever said, "My only regret is that I did not spend more time at the office." People often regret not spending more time with their family or increasing their knowledge. We pray and hope to live long. We should live our days so that we will be able to enjoy recalling the past. A lesson in proper living for us all.

SUGGESTIONS FOR FURTHER READING

Canfield, Jack, et al. *Six Pillars of Self-Esteem*. New York: Bantam, 1994.

———. *Chicken Soup for the Couple's Soul*. Deerfield Beach, FL: Health Communications, 1999.

———. *Chicken Soup for the Girl's Soul*. Deerfield Beach, FL: Health Communications, 2005.

———. *Chicken Soup for the Grandparent's Soul*. Deerfield Beach, FL: Health Communications, 2004.

———. *Chicken Soup for the Prisoner's Soul*. Deerfield Beach, FL: Health Communications, 2002.

———. *Chicken Soup for the Recovering Soul*. Deerfield Beach, FL: Health Communications, 2004.

———. *Chicken Soup for the Teenage Soul*. Deerfield Beach, FL: Health Communications, 1997.

———. *Living Your Dreams*. Deerfield Beach, FL: Health Communications, 2003.

Chopra, Deepak. *The Seven Spiritual Laws of Success*. Novato, CA: New World Library, 1994.

Clarke, Jean Illsley. *Self-Esteem: A Family Affair*. Center City, MN: Hazelden, 1998.

Dessler, Eliyahu. *Strive for Truth*. Vols. 1–3. New York: Feldheim, 2004.

Elkins, Dov Peretz. *Jewish Stories from Heaven and Earth: Inspiring Tales to Nourish the Heart and Soul*. Woodstock, VT: Jewish Lights, 2008.

Frankl, Viktor. *Man's Search for Meaning*. (Written in 1945 and first published in English, by Beacon Press, in 1959; many editions have been released since then.)

Gill, Brendan. *Late Bloomers*. New York: Workman/Artisan, 1998.

Kedar, Karyn D. *The Bridge to Forgiveness: Stories and Prayers for Finding God and Restoring Wholeness*. Woodstock, VT: Jewish Lights, 2007.

———. *God Whispers: Stories of the Soul, Lessons of the Heart*. Woodstock, VT: Jewish Lights, 2000.

———. *Our Dance with God: Finding Prayer, Perspective and Meaning in the Stories of Our Lives*. Woodstock, VT: Jewish Lights, 2004.

Kelly, Matthew. *The Rhythm of Life*. New York: Simon & Schuster, 1999.

Kurtz, Ernest, and Katherine Ketcham. *The Spirituality of Imperfection*. New York: Bantam Books, 1992.

Luzzatto, Moshe Chaim. *The Path of the Just*. Translated by Yosef Liebler. New York: Feldheim, 2004.

Olitzky, Kerry M. *Life's Daily Blessings: Inspiring Reflections on Gratitude and Joy for Every Day, Based on Jewish Wisdom*. Woodstock, VT: Jewish Lights, 2009.

Remen, Rachel Naomi. *Kitchen Table Wisdom*. New York: Riverhead Books, 1996.

———. *My Grandfather's Blessings*. New York: Riverhead Books, 2000.

Shapiro, Rami. *The Sacred Art of Lovingkindness: Preparing to Practice*. Woodstock, VT: SkyLight Paths, 2006.

Spitz, Elie Kaplan. *Healing from Despair: Choosing Wholeness in a Broken World*. With Erica Shapiro Taylor. Woodstock, VT: Jewish Lights, 2008.

Telushkin, Joseph. *The Book of Jewish Values: A Day-by-Day Guide to Ethical Living*. New York: Bell Tower, 2000.

———. *The Code of Jewish Ethics: You Shall Be Holy*. Vol. 1. New York: Bell Tower, 2006.

———. *The Code of Jewish Ethics: Love Your Neighbor*. Vol. 2. New York: Bell Tower, 2009.

Twerski, Abraham J. *Happiness and the Human Spirit: The Spirituality of Becoming the Best You Can Be*. Woodstock, VT: Jewish Lights, 2009.

———. *The Spiritual Self*. Center City, MN: Hazelden, 2000.

Bar/Bat Mitzvah

The JGirl's Guide: The Young Jewish Woman's Handbook for Coming of Age
By Penina Adelman, Ali Feldman, and Shulamit Reinharz
This inspirational, interactive guidebook helps pre-teen Jewish girls address the many
issues surrounding coming of age.   6 x 9, 240 pp, Quality PB, 978-1-58023-215-9 **$14.99**
   Also Available: **The JGirl's Teacher's and Parent's Guide**
   8½ x 11, 56 pp, PB, 978-1-58023-225-8 **$8.99**

Bar/Bat Mitzvah Basics: A Practical Family Guide to Coming of Age Together
   Edited by Cantor Helen Leneman   6 x 9, 240 pp, Quality PB, 978-1-58023-151-0 **$18.95**
The Bar/Bat Mitzvah Memory Book, 2nd Edition: An Album for Treasuring the
   Spiritual Celebration *By Rabbi Jeffrey K. Salkin and Nina Salkin*
   8 x 10, 48 pp, Deluxe HC, 2-color text, ribbon marker, 978-1-58023-263-0 **$19.99**
For Kids—Putting God on Your Guest List, 2nd Edition: How to Claim the
   Spiritual Meaning of Your Bar or Bat Mitzvah *By Rabbi Jeffrey K. Salkin*
   6 x 9, 144 pp, Quality PB, 978-1-58023-308-8 **$15.99** *For ages 11–13*

Putting God on the Guest List, 3rd Edition: How to Reclaim the Spiritual
   Meaning of Your Child's Bar or Bat Mitzvah *By Rabbi Jeffrey K. Salkin*
   6 x 9, 224 pp, Quality PB, 978-1-58023-222-7 **$16.99**; HC, 978-1-58023-260-9 **$24.99**
   Also Available: **Putting God on the Guest List Teacher's Guide**
   8½ x 11, 48 pp, PB, 978-1-58023-226-5 **$8.99**
Tough Questions Jews Ask: A Young Adult's Guide to Building a Jewish Life
   By Rabbi Edward Feinstein   6 x 9, 160 pp, Quality PB, 978-1-58023-139-8 **$14.99** *For ages 12 & up*
   Also Available: **Tough Questions Jews Ask Teacher's Guide**
   8½ x 11, 72 pp, PB, 978-1-58023-187-9 **$8.95**

Bible Study/Midrash

The Modern Men's Torah Commentary: New Insights from Jewish
Men on the 54 Weekly Torah Portions *Edited by Rabbi Jeffrey K. Salkin*
A major contribution to modern biblical commentary. Addresses the most important concerns of *modern* men by opening them up to the life of Torah.
6 x 9, 368 pp, HC, 978-1-58023-395-8 **$24.99**

The Genesis of Leadership: What the Bible Teaches Us about Vision,
Values and Leading Change *By Rabbi Nathan Laufer; Foreword by Senator Joseph I. Lieberman*
Unlike other books on leadership, this one is rooted in the stories of the Bible.
6 x 9, 288 pp, Quality PB, 978-1-58023-352-1 **$18.99**; HC, 978-1-58023-241-8 **$24.99**

Hineini in Our Lives: Learning How to Respond to Others through 14 Biblical Texts
   and Personal Stories *By Norman J. Cohen*   6 x 9, 240 pp, Quality PB, 978-1-58023-274-6 **$16.99**
Moses and the Journey to Leadership: Timeless Lessons of Effective Management from
   the Bible and Today's Leaders *By Dr. Norman J. Cohen*
   6 x 9, 240 pp, Quality PB, 978-1-58023-351-4 **$18.99**; HC, 978-1-58023-227-2 **$21.99**
Self, Struggle & Change: Family Conflict Stories in Genesis and Their Healing Insights for
   Our Lives *By Norman J. Cohen*   6 x 9, 224 pp, Quality PB, 978-1-879045-66-8 **$18.99**

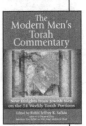

The Triumph of Eve & Other Subversive Bible Tales *By Matt Biers-Ariel*
   5½ x 8½, 192 pp, Quality PB, 978-1-59473-176-1 **$14.99**; HC, 978-1-59473-040-5 **$19.99**
   (A book from SkyLight Paths, Jewish Lights' sister imprint)
The Wisdom of Judaism: An Introduction to the Values of the Talmud
By Rabbi Dov Peretz Elkins
Explores the essence of Judaism.   6 x 9, 192 pp, Quality PB, 978-1-58023-327-9 **$16.99**
   Also Available: **The Wisdom of Judaism Teacher's Guide**
   8½ x 11, 18 pp, PB, 978-1-58023-350-7 **$8.99**

Or phone, fax, mail or e-mail to: **JEWISH LIGHTS Publishing**
Sunset Farm Offices, Route 4 • P.O. Box 237 • Woodstock, Vermont 05091
Tel: (802) 457-4000 • Fax: (802) 457-4004 • www.jewishlights.com
Credit card orders: **(800) 962-4544** (8:30AM–5:30PM ET Monday–Friday)
Generous discounts on quantity orders. SATISFACTION GUARANTEED. Prices subject to change.

Current Events/History

A Dream of Zion: American Jews Reflect on Why Israel Matters to Them
Edited by Rabbi Jeffrey K. Salkin Explores what Jewish people in America have to say
about Israel. 6 x 9, 304 pp, Quality PB, 978-1-58023-415-3 **$18.99**; HC, 978-1-58023-340-8 **$24.99**
Also Available: **A Dream of Zion Teacher's Guide** 8½ x 11, 32 pp, PB, 978-1-58023-356-9 **$8.99**

The Jewish Connection to Israel, the Promised Land: A Brief Introduction for
Christians *By Rabbi Eugene Korn, PhD* 5½ x 8½, 192 pp, Quality PB, 978-1-58023-318-7 **$14.99**

The Story of the Jews: A 4,000-Year Adventure—A Graphic History Book
Written & illustrated by Stan Mack 6 x 9, 288 pp, illus., Quality PB, 978-1-58023-155-8 **$16.99**

Hannah Senesh: Her Life and Diary, the First Complete Edition
By Hannah Senesh; Foreword by Marge Piercy; Preface by Eitan Senesh; Afterword by Roberta Grossman
6 x 9, 368 pp, b/w photos, Quality PB, 978-1-58023-342-2 **$19.99**

The Ethiopian Jews of Israel: Personal Stories of Life in the Promised
Land *By Len Lyons, PhD; Foreword by Alan Dershowitz; Photographs by Ilan Ossendryver*
Recounts, through photographs and words, stories of Ethiopian Jews.
10½ x 10, 240 pp, 100 full-color photos, HC, 978-1-58023-323-1 **$34.99**

Foundations of Sephardic Spirituality: The Inner Life of Jews of the Ottoman Empire
By Rabbi Marc D. Angel, PhD 6 x 9, 224 pp, Quality PB, 978-1-58023-341-5 **$18.99**

Judaism and Justice: The Jewish Passion to Repair the World
By Rabbi Sidney Schwarz 6 x 9, 352 pp, Quality PB, 978-1-58023-353-8 **$19.99**

Ecology/Environment

A Wild Faith: Jewish Ways into Wilderness, Wilderness Ways into Judaism
By Rabbi Mike Comins; Foreword by Nigel Savage
Offers ways to enliven and deepen your spiritual life through wilderness experience.
6 x 9, 240 pp, Quality PB, 978-1-58023-316-3 **$16.99**

Ecology & the Jewish Spirit: Where Nature & the Sacred Meet
Edited by Ellen Bernstein 6 x 9, 288 pp, Quality PB, 978-1-58023-082-7 **$18.99**

Torah of the Earth: Exploring 4,000 Years of Ecology in Jewish Thought
Vol. 1: Biblical Israel: One Land, One People; Rabbinic Judaism: One People, Many Lands
Vol. 2: Zionism: One Land, Two Peoples; Eco-Judaism: One Earth, Many Peoples
Edited by Arthur Waskow Vol. 1: 6 x 9, 272 pp, Quality PB, 978-1-58023-086-5 **$19.95**
Vol. 2: 6 x 9, 336 pp, Quality PB, 978-1-58023-087-2 **$19.95**

The Way Into Judaism and the Environment *By Jeremy Benstein, PhD*
6 x 9, 288 pp, Quality PB, 978-1-58023-368-2 **$18.99**; HC, 978-1-58023-268-5 **$24.99**

Grief/Healing

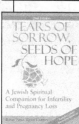

Healing and the Jewish Imagination: Spiritual and Practical
Perspectives on Judaism and Health *Edited by Rabbi William Cutter, PhD*
Explores Judaism for comfort in times of illness and perspectives on suffering.
6 x 9, 240 pp, Quality PB, 978-1-58023-373-6 **$19.99**; HC, 978-1-58023-314-9 **$24.99**

Grief in Our Seasons: A Mourner's Kaddish Companion *By Rabbi Kerry M. Olitzky*
4½ x 6½, 448 pp, Quality PB, 978-1-879045-55-2 **$15.95**

Healing of Soul, Healing of Body: Spiritual Leaders Unfold the Strength & Solace
in Psalms *Edited by Rabbi Simkha Y. Weintraub, CSW*
6 x 9, 128 pp, 2-color illus. text, Quality PB, 978-1-879045-31-6 **$14.99**

Mourning & Mitzvah, 2nd Edition: A Guided Journal for Walking the Mourner's
Path through Grief to Healing *By Anne Brener, LCSW*
7½ x 9, 304 pp, Quality PB, 978-1-58023-113-8 **$19.99**

Tears of Sorrow, Seeds of Hope, 2nd Edition: A Jewish Spiritual Companion for
Infertility and Pregnancy Loss *By Rabbi Nina Beth Cardin*
6 x 9, 208 pp, Quality PB, 978-1-58023-233-3 **$18.99**

A Time to Mourn, a Time to Comfort, 2nd Edition: A Guide to Jewish
Bereavement *By Dr. Ron Wolfson*
7 x 9, 384 pp, Quality PB, 978-1-58023-253-1 **$19.99**

When a Grandparent Dies: A Kid's Own Remembering Workbook for Dealing
with Shiva and the Year Beyond *By Nechama Liss-Levinson, PhD*
8 x 10, 48 pp, 2-color text, HC, 978-1-879045-44-6 **$15.95** *For ages 7–13*

Spirituality

Journeys to a Jewish Life: Inspiring Stories from the Spiritual Journeys of American Jews *By Paula Amann*
Examines the soul treks of Jews lost and found. 6 x 9, 208 pp, HC, 978-1-58023-317-0 **$19.99**

The Adventures of Rabbi Harvey: A Graphic Novel of Jewish Wisdom and Wit in the Wild West *By Steve Sheinkin*
Jewish and American folktales combine in this witty and original graphic novel collection. Creatively retold and set on the western frontier of the 1870s.
6 x 9, 144 pp, Full-color illus., Quality PB, 978-1-58023-310-1 **$16.99**

Rabbi Harvey Rides Again
A Graphic Novel of Jewish Folktales Let Loose in the Wild West *By Steve Sheinkin*
6 x 9, 144 pp, Quality PB Original, Full-color illus., 978-1-58023-347-7 **$16.99**

Ethics of the Sages: *Pirke Avot*—Annotated & Explained
Translation and Annotation by Rabbi Rami Shapiro 5½ x 8½, 192 pp, Quality PB, 978-1-59473-207-2
$16.99 *(A book from SkyLight Paths, Jewish Lights' sister imprint)*

A Book of Life: Embracing Judaism as a Spiritual Practice
By Michael Strassfeld 6 x 9, 528 pp, Quality PB, 978-1-58023-247-0 **$19.99**

Meaning and Mitzvah: Daily Practices for Reclaiming Judaism through Prayer, God, Torah, Hebrew, Mitzvot and Peoplehood *By Rabbi Goldie Milgram*
7 x 9, 336 pp, Quality PB, 978-1-58023-256-2 **$19.99**

The Soul of the Story: Meetings with Remarkable People
By Rabbi David Zeller 6 x 9, 288 pp, HC, 978-1-58023-272-2 **$21.99**

Aleph-Bet Yoga: Embodying the Hebrew Letters for Physical and Spiritual Well-Being
By Steven A. Rapp. Foreword by Tamar Frankiel, PhD and Judy Greenfeld. Preface by Hart Lazer.
7 x 10, 128 pp, b/w photos, Quality PB, Layflat binding, 978-1-58023-162-6 **$16.95**

Does the Soul Survive? A Jewish Journey to Belief in Afterlife, Past Lives & Living with Purpose *By Rabbi Elie Kaplan Spitz; Foreword by Brian L. Weiss, MD*
6 x 9, 288 pp, Quality PB, 978-1-58023-165-7 **$16.99**

First Steps to a New Jewish Spirit: Reb Zalman's Guide to Recapturing the Intimacy & Ecstasy in Your Relationship with God *By Rabbi Zalman M. Schachter-Shalomi with Donald Gropman* 6 x 9, 144 pp, Quality PB, 978-1-58023-182-4 **$16.95**

God in Our Relationships: Spirituality between People from the Teachings of Martin Buber *By Rabbi Dennis S. Ross* 5½ x 8½, 160 pp, Quality PB, 978-1-58023-147-3 **$16.95**

Judaism, Physics and God: Searching for Sacred Metaphors in a Post-Einstein World
By Rabbi David W. Nelson 6 x 9, 368 pp, Quality PB, inc. reader's discussion guide, 978-1-58023-306-4 **$18.99**;
HC, 352 pp, 978-1-58023-252-4 **$24.99**

The Jewish Lights Spirituality Handbook: A Guide to Understanding, Exploring & Living a Spiritual Life *Edited by Stuart M. Matlins*
What exactly is "Jewish" about spirituality? How do I make it a part of my life? Fifty of today's foremost spiritual leaders share their ideas and experience with us.
6 x 9, 456 pp, Quality PB, 978-1-58023-093-3 **$19.99**

Bringing the Psalms to Life: How to Understand and Use the Book of Psalms
By Daniel F. Polish 6 x 9, 208 pp, Quality PB, 978-1-58023-157-2 **$16.95**;
HC, 978-1-58023-077-3 **$21.95**

God & the Big Bang: Discovering Harmony between Science & Spirituality
By Daniel C. Matt 6 x 9, 216 pp, Quality PB, 978-1-879045-89-7 **$16.99**

Minding the Temple of the Soul: Balancing Body, Mind, and Spirit through Traditional Jewish Prayer, Movement, and Meditation *By Tamar Frankiel, PhD, and Judy Greenfeld*
7 x 10, 184 pp, illus., Quality PB, 978-1-879045-64-4 **$16.95**

One God Clapping: The Spiritual Path of a Zen Rabbi *By Alan Lew with Sherril Jaffe*
5½ x 8½, 336 pp, Quality PB, 978-1-58023-115-2 **$16.95**

There Is No Messiah ... and You're It: The Stunning Transformation of Judaism's Most Provocative Idea *By Rabbi Robert N. Levine, DD*
6 x 9, 192 pp, Quality PB, 978-1-58023-255-5 **$16.99**

These Are the Words: A Vocabulary of Jewish Spiritual Life
By Arthur Green 6 x 9, 304 pp, Quality PB, 978-1-58023-107-7 **$18.95**

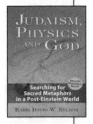

Theology/Philosophy

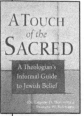

A Touch of the Sacred: A Theologian's Informal Guide to Jewish Belief
By Dr. Eugene B. Borowitz and Frances W. Schwartz
Explores the musings from the leading theologian of liberal Judaism.
6 x 9, 256 pp, Quality PB, 978-1-58023-416-0 **$16.99**; HC, 978-1-58023-337-8 **$21.99**

Talking about God: Exploring the Meaning of Religious Life with Kierkegaard, Buber, Tillich and Heschel *By Daniel F. Polish, PhD*
Examines the meaning of the human religious experience with the greatest theologians of modern times. 6 x 9, 160 pp, HC, 978-1-59473-230-0 **$21.99**
(A book from SkyLight Paths, Jewish Lights' sister imprint)

Jews & Judaism in the 21st Century: Human Responsibility, the Presence of God, and the Future of the Covenant *Edited by Rabbi Edward Feinstein; Foreword by Paula E. Hyman* Five celebrated leaders in Judaism examine contemporary Jewish life. 6 x 9, 192 pp, Quality PB, 978-1-58023-374-3 **$19.99**; HC, 978-1-58023-315-6 **$24.99**

Christians and Jews in Dialogue: Learning in the Presence of the Other
By Mary C. Boys and Sara S. Lee; Foreword by Dr. Dorothy Bass
6 x 9, 240 pp, Quality PB, 978-1-59473-254-6 **$18.99**; HC, 978-1-59473-144-0 **$21.99**
(A book from SkyLight Paths, Jewish Lights' sister imprint)

The Death of Death: Resurrection and Immortality in Jewish Thought
By Neil Gillman 6 x 9, 336 pp, Quality PB, 978-1-58023-081-0 **$18.95**

Ethics of the Sages: Pirke Avot—Annotated & Explained
Translation & Annotation by Rabbi Rami Shapiro
5½ x 8¼, 208 pp, Quality PB, 978-1-59473-207-2 **$16.99** *(A book from SkyLight Paths, Jewish Lights' sister imprint)*

Hasidic Tales: Annotated & Explained *By Rabbi Rami Shapiro; Foreword by Andrew Harvey*
5½ x 8¼, 240 pp, Quality PB, 978-1-893361-86-7 **$16.95** *(A book from SkyLight Paths, Jewish Lights' sister imprint)*

A Heart of Many Rooms: Celebrating the Many Voices within Judaism
By David Hartman 6 x 9, 352 pp, Quality PB, 978-1-58023-156-5 **$19.95**

The Hebrew Prophets: Selections Annotated & Explained
Translation & Annotation by Rabbi Rami Shapiro; Foreword by Zalman M. Schachter-Shalomi
5½ x 8¼, 224 pp, Quality PB, 978-1-59473-037-5 **$16.99** *(A book from SkyLight Paths, Jewish Lights' sister imprint)*

A Jewish Understanding of the New Testament
By Rabbi Samuel Sandmel; Preface by Rabbi David Sandmel
5½ x 8¼, 368 pp, Quality PB, 978-1-59473-048-1 **$19.99** *(A book from SkyLight Paths, Jewish Lights' sister imprint)*

Keeping Faith with the Psalms: Deepen Your Relationship with God Using the Book of Psalms *By Daniel F. Polish* 6 x 9, 320 pp, Quality PB, 978-1-58023-300-2 **$18.99**

A Living Covenant: The Innovative Spirit in Traditional Judaism
By David Hartman 6 x 9, 368 pp, Quality PB, 978-1-58023-011-7 **$20.00**

Love and Terror in the God Encounter: The Theological Legacy of Rabbi Joseph B. Soloveitchik *By David Hartman* 6 x 9, 240 pp, Quality PB, 978-1-58023-176-3 **$19.95**

The Personhood of God: Biblical Theology, Human Faith and the Divine Image
By Dr. Yochanan Muffs; Foreword by Dr. David Hartman
6 x 9, 240 pp, Quality PB, 978-1-58023-338-5 **$18.99**; HC, 978-1-58023-265-4 **$24.99**

Traces of God: Seeing God in Torah, History and Everyday Life *By Neil Gillman*
6 x 9, 240 pp, Quality PB, 978-1-58023-369-9 **$16.99**; HC, 978-1-58023-249-4 **$21.99**

We Jews and Jesus: Exploring Theological Differences for Mutual Understanding
By Rabbi Samuel Sandmel; Preface by Rabbi David Sandmel
6 x 9, 176 pp, Quality PB, 978-1-59473-208-9 **$16.99** *(A book from SkyLight Paths, Jewish Lights' sister imprint)*

Your Word Is Fire: The Hasidic Masters on Contemplative Prayer
Edited and translated by Arthur Green and Barry W. Holtz
6 x 9, 160 pp, Quality PB, 978-1-879045-25-5 **$15.95**

I Am Jewish
Personal Reflections Inspired by the Last Words of Daniel Pearl
Almost 150 Jews—both famous and not—from all walks of life, from all around the world, write about many aspects of their Judaism.
Edited by Judea and Ruth Pearl 6 x 9, 304 pp, Deluxe PB w/flaps, 978-1-58023-259-3 **$18.99**
Download a free copy of the *I Am Jewish Teacher's Guide* at our website:
www.jewishlights.com

Social Justice

There Shall Be No Needy
Pursuing Social Justice through Jewish Law and Tradition
By Rabbi Jill Jacobs; Foreword by Rabbi Elliot N. Dorff, PhD; Preface by Simon Greer
Confronts the most pressing issues of twenty-first-century America from a deeply Jewish perspective.
6 x 9, 288 pp, HC, 978-1-58023-394-1 **$21.99**

Conscience: The Duty to Obey and the Duty to Disobey
By Rabbi Harold M. Schulweis
This clarion call to rethink our moral and political behavior examines the idea of conscience and the role conscience plays in our relationships to governments, law, ethics, religion, human nature, God—and to each other.
6 x 9, 160 pp, HC, 978-1-58023-375-0 **$19.99**

Judaism and Justice: The Jewish Passion to Repair the World
By Rabbi Sidney Schwarz; Foreword by Ruth Messinger
Explores the relationship between Judaism, social justice and the Jewish identity of American Jews.
6 x 9, 352 pp, Quality PB, 978-1-58023-353-8 **$19.99**; HC, 978-1-58023-312-5 **$24.99**

Spiritual Activism: A Jewish Guide to Leadership and Repairing the World
By Rabbi Avraham Weiss; Foreword by Alan M. Dershowitz
6 x 9, 224 pp, HC, 978-1-58023-355-2 **$24.99**

Righteous Indignation: A Jewish Call for Justice
Edited by Rabbi Or N. Rose, Jo Ellen Green Kaiser and Margie Klein; Foreword by Rabbi David Ellenson
Leading progressive Jewish activists explore meaningful intellectual and spiritual foundations for their social justice work.
6 x 9, 384 pp, Quality PB, 978-1-58023-414-6 **$19.99**; HC, 978-1-58023-336-1 **$24.99**

Spirituality/Women's Interest

New Jewish Feminism: Probing the Past, Forging the Future
Edited by Rabbi Elyse Goldstein; Foreword by Anita Diamant
Looks at the growth and accomplishments of Jewish feminism and what that means for Jewish women today and tomorrow.
6 x 9, 480 pp, HC, 978-1-58023-359-0 **$24.99**

The Quotable Jewish Woman: Wisdom, Inspiration & Humor from the Mind & Heart
Edited and compiled by Elaine Bernstein Partnow
6 x 9, 496 pp, Quality PB, 978-1-58023-236-4 **$19.99**; HC, 978-1-58023-193-0 **$29.99**

The Divine Feminine in Biblical Wisdom Literature
Selections Annotated & Explained
Translated and Annotated by Rabbi Rami Shapiro
5½ x 8½, 240 pp, Quality PB, 978-1-59473-109-9 **$16.99**
(A book from SkyLight Paths, Jewish Lights' sister imprint)

The Women's Haftarah Commentary: New Insights from Women Rabbis on the 54 Weekly Haftarah Portions, the 5 Megillot & Special Shabbatot
Edited by Rabbi Elyse Goldstein
Illuminates the historical significance of female portrayals in the Haftarah and the Five Megillot.
6 x 9, 560 pp, Quality PB, 978-1-58023-371-2 **$19.99**; HC, 978-1-58023-133-6 **$39.99**

The Women's Torah Commentary: New Insights from Women Rabbis on the 54 Weekly Torah Portions
Edited by Rabbi Elyse Goldstein
Over fifty women rabbis offer inspiring insights on the Torah, in a week-by-week format.
6 x 9, 496 pp, Quality PB, 978-1-58023-370-5 **$19.99**; HC, 978-1-58023-076-6 **$34.95**

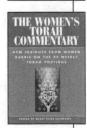

Spirituality/Lawrence Kushner

Filling Words with Light: Hasidic and Mystical Reflections on Jewish Prayer
By Lawrence Kushner and Nehemia Polen
5½ x 8½, 176 pp, Quality PB, 978-1-58023-238-8 **$16.99**; HC, 978-1-58023-216-6 **$21.99**

The Book of Letters: A Mystical Hebrew Alphabet
Popular HC Edition, 6 x 9, 80 pp, 2-color text, 978-1-879045-00-2 **$24.95**
Collector's Limited Edition, 9 x 12, 80 pp, gold foil embossed pages, w/limited edition silkscreened print, 978-1-879045-04-0 **$349.00**

The Book of Miracles: A Young Person's Guide to Jewish Spiritual Awareness
6 x 9, 96 pp, 2-color illus., HC, 978-1-879045-78-1 **$16.95** *For ages 9 and up*

The Book of Words: Talking Spiritual Life, Living Spiritual Talk
6 x 9, 160 pp, Quality PB, 978-1-58023-020-9 **$16.95**

Eyes Remade for Wonder: A Lawrence Kushner Reader *Introduction by Thomas Moore*
6 x 9, 240 pp, Quality PB, 978-1-58023-042-1 **$18.95**

God Was in This Place & I, i Did Not Know: Finding Self, Spirituality and
Ultimate Meaning 6 x 9, 192 pp, Quality PB, 978-1-879045-33-0 **$16.95**

Honey from the Rock: An Introduction to Jewish Mysticism
6 x 9, 176 pp, Quality PB, 978-1-58023-073-5 **$16.95**

Invisible Lines of Connection: Sacred Stories of the Ordinary
5½ x 8½, 160 pp, Quality PB, 978-1-879045-98-9 **$15.95**

Jewish Spirituality—A Brief Introduction for Christians
5½ x 8½, 112 pp, Quality PB, 978-1-58023-150-3 **$12.95**

The River of Light: Jewish Mystical Awareness
6 x 9, 192 pp, Quality PB, 978-1-58023-096-4 **$16.95**

The Way Into Jewish Mystical Tradition
6 x 9, 224 pp, Quality PB, 978-1-58023-200-5 **$18.99**; HC, 978-1-58023-029-2 **$21.95**

Spirituality/Prayer

My People's Passover Haggadah: Traditional Texts, Modern Commentaries
Edited by Rabbi Lawrence A. Hoffman, PhD, and David Arnow, PhD Diverse commentaries
on the traditional Passover Haggadah—in two volumes! Vol. 1: 7 x 10, 304 pp, HC
978-1-58023-354-5 **$24.99** Vol. 2: 7 x 10, 320 pp, HC, 978-1-58023-346-0 **$24.99**

Witnesses to the One: The Spiritual History of the *Sh'ma* By Rabbi Joseph B.
Meszler; Foreword by Rabbi Elyse Goldstein 6 x 9, 176 pp, HC, 978-1-58023-309-5 **$19.99**

My People's Prayer Book Series
Traditional Prayers, Modern Commentaries *Edited by Rabbi Lawrence A. Hoffman*
Provides diverse and exciting commentary to the traditional liturgy, helping modern
men and women find new wisdom in Jewish prayer, and bring liturgy into their lives.
Each book includes Hebrew text, modern translation, and commentaries from all
perspectives of the Jewish world.

Vol. 1—The *Sh'ma* and Its Blessings
7 x 10, 168 pp, HC, 978-1-879045-79-8 **$24.99**
Vol. 2—The *Amidah*
7 x 10, 240 pp, HC, 978-1-879045-80-4 **$24.95**
Vol. 3—*P'sukei D'zimrah* (Morning Psalms)
7 x 10, 240 pp, HC, 978-1-879045-81-1 **$24.95**
Vol. 4—*Seder K'riat Hatorah* (The Torah Service)
7 x 10, 264 pp, HC, 978-1-879045-82-8 **$23.95**
Vol. 5—*Birkhot Hashachar* (Morning Blessings)
7 x 10, 240 pp, HC, 978-1-879045-83-5 **$24.95**
Vol. 6—*Tachanun* and Concluding Prayers
7 x 10, 240 pp, HC, 978-1-879045-84-2 **$24.95**
Vol. 7—Shabbat at Home
7 x 10, 240 pp, HC, 978-1-879045-85-9 **$24.95**
Vol. 8—*Kabbalat Shabbat* (Welcoming Shabbat in the Synagogue)
7 x 10, 240 pp, HC, 978-1-58023-121-3 **$24.99**
Vol. 9—Welcoming the Night: *Minchah* and *Ma'ariv* (Afternoon and
Evening Prayer) 7 x 10, 272 pp, HC, 978-1-58023-262-3 **$24.99**
Vol. 10—Shabbat Morning: *Shacharit* and *Musaf* (Morning and
Additional Services) 7 x 10, 240 pp, HC, 978-1-58023-240-1 **$24.99**

Inspiration

The Seven Questions You're Asked in Heaven: Reviewing and
Renewing Your Life on Earth *By Dr. Ron Wolfson*
An intriguing and entertaining resource for living a life that matters.
6 x 9, 176 pp, Quality PB, 978-1-58023-407-8 **$16.99**

Happiness and the Human Spirit: The Spirituality of Becoming the
Best You Can Be *By Abraham J. Twerski, MD*
Shows you that true happiness is attainable once you stop looking outside yourself for
the source. 6 x 9, 176 pp, Quality PB, 978-1-58023-404-7 **$16.99**; HC, 978-1-58023-343-9 **$19.99**

Life's Daily Blessings: Inspiring Reflections on Gratitude and Joy for Every Day, Based on
Jewish Wisdom *By Rabbi Kerry M. Olitzky* 4½ x 6½, 368 pp, Quality PB, 978-1-58023-396-5 **$16.99**

The Bridge to Forgiveness: Stories and Prayers for Finding God and
Restoring Wholeness *By Rabbi Karyn D. Kedar*
Examines how forgiveness can be the bridge that connects us to wholeness and peace.
6 x 9, 176 pp, HC, 978-1-58023-324-8 **$19.99**

God's To-Do List: 103 Ways to Be an Angel and Do God's Work on Earth
By Dr. Ron Wolfson 6 x 9, 150 pp, Quality PB, 978-1-58023-301-9 **$16.99**

Our Dance with God: Finding Prayer, Perspective and Meaning in the Stories of Our
Lives *By Karyn D. Kedar* 6 x 9, 176 pp, Quality PB, 978-1-58023-202-9 **$16.99**
Also Available: **The Dance of the Dolphin** (HC edition of Our Dance with God)
6 x 9, 176 pp, HC, 978-1-58023-202-9 **$19.95**

The Empty Chair: Finding Hope and Joy—Timeless Wisdom from a Hasidic Master,
Rebbe Nachman of Breslov *Adapted by Moshe Mykoff and the Breslov Research Institute*
4 x 6, 128 pp, Deluxe PB w/flaps, 978-1-879045-67-5 **$9.99**

The Gentle Weapon: Prayers for Everyday and Not-So-Everyday Moments—
Timeless Wisdom from the Teachings of the Hasidic Master, Rebbe Nachman of Breslov
Adapted by Moshe Mykoff and S. C. Mizrahi, together with the Breslov Research Institute
4 x 6, 144 pp, Deluxe PB w/flaps, 978-1-58023-022-3 **$9.99**

God Whispers: Stories of the Soul, Lessons of the Heart *By Karyn D. Kedar*
6 x 9, 176 pp, Quality PB, 978-1-58023-088-9 **$15.95**

Restful Reflections: Nighttime Inspiration to Calm the Soul, Based on Jewish Wisdom
By Rabbi Kerry M. Olitzky & Rabbi Lori Forman 4½ x 6½, 448 pp, Quality PB, 978-1-58023-091-9 **$15.95**

Sacred Intentions: Daily Inspiration to Strengthen the Spirit, Based on Jewish Wisdom
By Rabbi Kerry M. Olitzky and Rabbi Lori Forman 4½ x 6½, 448 pp, Quality PB, 978-1-58023-061-2 **$15.95**

Kabbalah/Mysticism

Seek My Face: A Jewish Mystical Theology *By Arthur Green*
6 x 9, 304 pp, Quality PB, 978-1-58023-130-5 **$19.95**

Zohar: Annotated & Explained *Translation and annotation by Daniel C. Matt; Foreword by
Andrew Harvey* 5½ x 8½, 176 pp, Quality PB, 978-1-893361-51-5 **$15.99**
(A book from SkyLight Paths, Jewish Lights' sister imprint)

Ehyeh: A Kabbalah for Tomorrow
By Arthur Green 6 x 9, 224 pp, Quality PB, 978-1-58023-213-5 **$16.99**

The Flame of the Heart: Prayers of a Chasidic Mystic *By Reb Noson of Breslov. Translated by
David Sears with the Breslov Research Institute* 5 x 7¼, 160 pp, Quality PB, 978-1-58023-246-3 **$15.99**

The Gift of Kabbalah: Discovering the Secrets of Heaven, Renewing Your Life on Earth
By Tamar Frankiel, PhD 6 x 9, 256 pp, Quality PB, 978-1-58023-141-1 **$16.95**
HC, 978-1-58023-108-4 **$21.95**

Kabbalah: A Brief Introduction for Christians
By Tamar Frankiel, PhD 5½ x 8½, 208 pp, Quality PB, 978-1-58023-303-3 **$16.99**

The Lost Princess and Other Kabbalistic Tales of Rebbe Nachman of Breslov
The Seven Beggars and Other Kabbalistic Tales of Rebbe Nachman of Breslov
Translated by Rabbi Aryeh Kaplan; Preface by Rabbi Chaim Kramer
Lost Princess: 6 x 9, 400 pp, Quality PB, 978-1-58023-217-3 **$18.99**
Seven Beggars: 6 x 9, 192 pp, Quality PB, 978-1-58023-250-0 **$16.99**

About Jewish Lights

People of all faiths and backgrounds yearn for books that attract, engage, educate, and spiritually inspire.

Our principal goal is to stimulate thought and help all people learn about who the Jewish People are, where they come from, and what the future can be made to hold. While people of our diverse Jewish heritage are the primary audience, our books speak to people in the Christian world as well and will broaden their understanding of Judaism and the roots of their own faith.

We bring to you authors who are at the forefront of spiritual thought and experience. While each has something different to say, they all say it in a voice that you can hear.

Our books are designed to welcome you and then to engage, stimulate, and inspire. We judge our success not only by whether or not our books are beautiful and commercially successful, but by whether or not they make a difference in your life.

For your information and convenience, at the back of this book we have provided a list of other Jewish Lights books you might find interesting and useful. They cover all the categories of your life:

Bar/Bat Mitzvah	Life Cycle
Bible Study / Midrash	Meditation
Children's Books	Men's Interest
Congregation Resources	Parenting
Current Events / History	Prayer / Ritual / Sacred Practice
Ecology / Environment	Social Justice
Fiction: Mystery, Science Fiction	Spirituality
Grief / Healing	Theology / Philosophy
Holidays / Holy Days	Travel
Inspiration	12-Step
Kabbalah / Mysticism / Enneagram	Women's Interest

Stuart M. Matlins, Publisher

Or phone, fax, mail or e-mail to: **JEWISH LIGHTS Publishing**
Sunset Farm Offices, Route 4 • P.O. Box 237 • Woodstock, Vermont 05091
Tel: (802) 457-4000 • Fax: (802) 457-4004 • www.jewishlights.com
Credit card orders: **(800) 962-4544** (8:30AM–5:30PM ET Monday–Friday)
Generous discounts on quantity orders. SATISFACTION GUARANTEED. Prices subject to change.

For more information about each book, visit our website at www.jewishlights.com

Printed in the USA
CPSIA information can be obtained
at www.ICGtesting.com
JSHW012037140824
68134JS00033B/3106